MW01194821

"When We Were Young"

D. Milan

ISBN-13:978-151425605

FOREWORD

I realized something. To really start this project, it took an immersion; an introspective journey that required attention. care, and time. I had to fall in love with writing, likening to the rebirth of a Phoenix.

Be open.

Be honest.

Unapologetically me.

I've been compelled to tell this story many times before. Suppose it wasn't my season. Timing. In my 25th year, I chose to accept the responsibility of the gift bestowed upon me; upon us all. We all have something to offer; that special, undeniable quality that separates us from the rest. Upon its awakening, for those who choose to answer its call, a sensation becomes infused into our being, our essence. It permeates our actions and plagues our thoughts. For those of us who are blessed to know the exhilaration of passion, it is our duty to allow that light to live within us, illuminating the path before us; aware that our light is the beacon for those still searching.

It is important to know that this did not come without fear; without consequence or sacrifice. No notion has ever been more fictitious. Maybe it is important for you to know.

I do feel, however, you should know this.

This is not a plea for understanding.

This is not meant for explanation, excuse, or egocentrism.

It is only...a story. A tale of triumph and tragedy through the lens of the misguided. The epic of the underdog. We all have a purpose. In my 25th year, I chose to walk in my own.

PRELUDE

Now Playing: Sherane a.k.a Master Splinters Daughter x Kendrick Lamar

Growing up was just that. Growing up. A cleared space against the foggy mirror of time. Memories muddled in mixtures of moments, mistaken realities. Never been one to lie or fabricate. I'm a country girl. Ask me where I'm from and I'll say a lot of places, but that really means the south. Small town Oklahoma. Smaller town Alabama. Small town colleges. Small town girl. The biggest city I ever lived in had three high schools. You never realize what home really looks like until you're gone.

I was a happy child. Never short on smiles, hugs, or an annoyingly sensible points on subjects much beyond my years. I was smart. Not that that was ever a selling point with my peers, but it was me. Young, bright, and full of personality. No bird could ever sing a sweeter song than the one my heart sang. Day in and out, there was a thirst for the acquisition of knowledge. Creativity loomed itself into my being at the first sound of noise. Organized noise woven into melodies that excited my soul; music. She was always there. Church choir, school choir, piano lessons -- the works. Harmonies had home in me as I learned the essence of octaves, the way music transcended every emotion, every being. I loved writing. Nothing ever came so naturally. The first writing competition I ever won was sponsored by a BGLO in my hometown. I was in the 3rd grade.

Sitting anxiously awaiting the winners, I sat in a gymnasium crowded full of people. It was an event for a sorority I had heard of. I didn't quite know what a sorority was, but I knew the colors were pretty and the very poised and pristine mother of a classmate had told my mom about it. *New Beginnings* was the name of my first work of fiction. It was a short about a young girl who had overcome a life of hardship to pursue her dreams.

Maybe this isn't my first time telling this story. Hindsight.

They asked Mrs. C, the woman who'd offered my invitation, to the stage to announce the winners. I remember looking as a spectator, as though I hadn't entered the competition myself. Congratulating the winners with enthused applause.

...then she called my name.

"1st place goes to..."

Blank.

Stage. Award. WAIT. WHAT?

There I was. The winner. Cheshire, ear to ear, I praised
myself for a victory I never set out to obtain. I just
wanted to write. Wanted someone to read it. Not only had
the *read* it, they *loved* it. Salutations held my family up
that night as everyone was eager to laud the child who
won.

It was a blur.

I just wanted to write.

Chapter 1

The story begins in a private, all-Black (except for that one time), Christian elementary school in southwest Oklahoma. We were a small school housed inside the annex building of the church across the street. Every morning we said the Pledge of Allegiance, the Pledge to the Christian Flag, and Pledge to the Bible. The corners of my little mind were crammed with passages, parables, and poems of empowerment. Coming up I learned about Black history; slavery, pioneers, role models, poets, dancers. It opened up a world of excellence and valor to me and created an admiration for my own. Although Oklahoma wasn't the most eventful place to grow up as a child, that rarely mattered. Writing, drawing, singing, were my outlets; anything that made my young heart free. And I loved to read. My imagination allowed the text to play in rich, vibrant colors.

During history lessons, I could almost feel the regal streets of Harlem in its reign; Black Hollywood. Many a night I spent dreaming of women who looked like me; gorgeous, desired, fabulous, smart. *Very* smart.

7th Grade circa 2004

Junior High was rough. Most everyone can agree. We've all had our run ins and altercations throughout our teens. I wasn't any exception to that rule. Tall and lanky with thick rimmed glasses twice the size of my face, I sported the best in thrift store couture. It was my first experience with public school, which meant my first time ever with my peers. Tennis shoes, always white, were my regular choice because, well...that's all I had. I didn't know much about doing my hair. This soon lead me into the drawstring ponytail trap.

You remember. The EXTRA shiny, SUPER bouncy ponytail that would attach to your own bound hair with the aid of conveniently hidden clips and, you guessed it, a drawstring. Between my threads, new do, and clean kicks, I was sure to do fine.

The world became a different place for me in those years. Prior to my entry into the "real world" the concept of ugly/pretty had not really existed, nor did dark/light. Imagine my surprise when I found out not only was I ugly but I was *dark.*
Tar Baby.

My new clothes only provided more ammunition for the other kids as I was perceived to be poor

especially since I NEVER had a new pair of those oh so nicely priced tennis shoes. It provided an added sense of worthlessness. I had come to my new school totally unarmed with the tools to handle what had come.

All of those poems of self love and worth I'd learned as a child, were met with the faces of people who said otherwise. And the faces, much like the poems, were real; however, nothing could expel the words that battered my soul. Real humans had spoken those words. Actual, living people. And it hurt. It damaged a portion of my spirit I'd not even known existed, until I felt it. Indescribable feelings of loneliness overwhelmed me day in and out as I struggled to accept that I just did NOT fit in.

I'd only managed to make two friends that year, but we were inseparable. I loved them dearly. They lived in the same neighborhood, so I would do my best to get over to their houses only for us to spend all day at the park talking about all the boys who had made passes at them.

One was a mixed Black girl; Bahamian and Black with killer hips and back dips to match. She was death to the idea that Black girls couldn't have long, pretty hair. The other was Chamoru (a native of Guam) with the most effortless urban style. By urban, I mean Black. All of her friends were Black, she was the captain of the step team, and she was the coolest girl in school, hands down. Braces and all. She was even dating one of the star football players (who later went on to a Division 1 program). And then…there was me. I was taller than them…by a lot, and I didn't have any cool credits to my name. No boyfriend. No booty. No bounty. Just nothing. But they never made me feel that way. When I was with them, I was one of the pretty girls because to them, I *was* pretty. Even though the only boys I was ever interested in had no idea I went to the same school as them and the ones who did always loudly laughed at me in the hallways when I would give my best attempt at the latest trends (i.e. jersey dresses). There wasn't much shape to fill out my clothes, so for most of the boys, I didn't exist. In an effort to quail my station in life, I joined the Academic Team. Honors courses were all I'd ever had, so when I was presented the opportunity to join the team I felt useful. I finally had an additive to my name. To no surprise, I was good. Biblical history and trivia were my strengths and I was the only girl on the team, so the spotlight was always on me. The collective of boys I'd had the pleasure of competing with were all in the same classes as me and all just as awkward. Mostly White, one Black, one with roots in India, and then me. We weren't unbeatable, but we sure were close and that made me feel worthy. Of what? Who knew? But I finally found a group of people who accepted me. They weren't going to laugh at me in the hallways because of what I was wearing or push me down any stairs. For once, I felt normal. The school year continued on as I started getting the hang of staying out of sight during class switches and lunch, getting to A-Team practice on time, and maintaining some type of average social life, even if that only meant waiting around a bit after school to spectate. The teasing was still constant, but I had learned to make less of a show of myself and to fly way, waaaayyy below the radar. Before I was able to begin my second year, my mother decided she wanted to be closer to her family. Barely finishing my first year of junior high, we prepared to pack up and move. Goodbyes were painful, but not as painful as what happened to me that first year. Black and ugly. That's all I would remember; the sounds of girls laughing, passing by my locker while I was only trying to get ready for gym; watching my friends get attention that I so desperately desired too.

When the conversation of moving was presented, I was ready. I was ready to start over, to try it all again. We left Oklahoma at the cusp of dark and dawn. I sat peering through the back windshield as the road disappeared behind me.

Chapter 2

I could always tell when we crossed the border of Mississippi and Alabama, even in a dead sleep. Beautiful, countryside air curtly interrupted by the smell of manure. The mixture of scents always alerted me to that special part of our trip. Both smells were comforting. Smelled familiar. That same familiarity reminded me of all of the holidays we spent at Granny's house; my cousins and I playing Spades on the back porch; sitting in Granddaddy's lap, because he always loved his *Slim Jim*, his *String Bean* and each time I swelled with joy as he told me how much he loved me, how pretty I was. I loved being in his presence. Great, big man with the voice of an angel. Oh, and Granddaddy loved to cook. Best sweet potato pie you could find for miles. Granddaddy was the first man to truly show me what it means to be loved.

How it's supposed to feel. And I loved him for that.

We moved into our home the summer of my 13th year. It was beautiful; a magnificent triple wide mobile home. One of the last of its kind. I had my own room and bathroom with a private entrance and a back porch that faced the road. Every day, solace came in the form of 18 wheelers wizzing up and down the highway. The countryside became my home. It seemed the only place in the world that felt that way. I guess because my family was there. The concepts of home and family never truly registered to me as it did with most. Many things left me wondering, how it was all really *supposed* to be. We were different. I had two dads, two sisters...sort of. Three. A brother? And growing up in the church made life all the more of a puzzle, but I figured I would learn it all at Home. Sweet Home, Alabama.

My first year in school there was unlike the year before. I was closer to my family than I ever. An 8-mile stretch and school rivalry separated us, but that never stopped me from scooting off to my aunt's house on the weekends or charming my way over to my great grandmother's house. How could anyone deny such a noble request? Not that I was off to any trouble. I just genuinely loved being around May Kate. I suppose I'd always gravitated towards the pillars of our family. Her calming strength and delicate demeanor soothed me on any given day. And May Kate never had a bad word for me, or anyone for that matter. She moved slow and spoke soft. *"Oh, you look so nice"* was her best compliment and it was one I looked forward to the most. I'd always made me examine my hair and clothes immediately wondering if she actually paid attention to that or had she been referring to some unknown quality about me. I never knew. But I did know, she meant it. So I accepted that.

--

The hallways were crowded with faces. New lockers, new classes, new people. The building was the shape of an open square; some classes were inside, others portables. The schedule took some getting used to, but the mornings were always the same. We were on a block schedule. But the day's start was consistent; music videos every morning from my favorite channels. My top four channels catered to all of my musical interests. The time spent flipping channels to avoid my awkward love of commercials benefited in my awakening to the outside world. The past year's encounters pushed me to learn more about others, why *I* was so different from them, and what other life lay beyond my frame of reference.

I spent my early teens enjoying the diversity of my new town. Well, diverse maybe isn't the term. But three things it certainly was....country, Black, and White. Everyone had grown up together. Same elementary schools, churches, family ties and everyone shared a common love of the south. Around that age, if color did matter, I didn't care. No notion that I wasn't aware. I simply enjoyed the company of *all* of my friends. We all loved four wheelers and country music. I hadn't grown up listening to country, but the lyrics always demonstrated their passion for life in its entirety. And I could respect that. Then I met a girl who introduced me to punk rock. I fell in love with the thunderous twangs of the strings, immersing myself in the angst that cried out from the hollowed voices that became my heaven. It felt nice to be understood. So many emotions rang out in those melodies that counseled those in me. Hurt, confusion, anger, love all expressed in a way that was new and dynamic. During that time, I truly developed a deeper understanding for music. It often occurred to me that I was a young, Black girl in the Deep South who loved country, hip hop, and punk rock. Confusing, yeah?

Yes. Very. Especially when you find yourself at the rear end of ridicule for it, in addition to host of other peculiarities.

Different. I'd always been that. And in that discovery I realized I would like what I liked, love what I loved, and the pain internally was enough to bear without questioning myself about the correlation between genre choice and skin color. I chose to openly relate to the vibe and the elements that created *good* music. My dad (stepdad) was a musician. He'd exposed me to classical music, jazz, gospel and funk when I was very young, so I just added my new loves to the catalog.

Middle school brought about the desire to make money, and music was my in. No particular need for the cash; I just enjoyed the freedom. I was making mixtapes long before they became a legitimate source of income. Literally, my locker would be stuffed with handwritten playlists from classmates, all of which equated to dollar signs to me. I loved giving people good music and the clientele was so varied! Students all over campus knew about my cds. It had to be one of the best kept secrets around. Of course, the administration and staff couldn't know because I could have been suspended or even expelled depending on how generous they felt. But, no one else was doing it. Plus, to ensure business I'd add a special touch, making sure to slide in a track or two from my favorite artists. There was a pleasure in exposing people to new sounds. They trusted me. Someone would always come back and say "*What was that last song on the cd? Who was that?*" every single time.

Friendship was easier too. I met my best friend that year. You know...the life long kind you go through all the stuff with and fight with...all that jazz? Well, we didn't do all of that. The delight of our relationship was in its simplicity. We liked sports, mainly basketball (she was better, I must admit). We liked music. We liked food. We made good grades. Simple. E was my shield, my comfort. She never judged me…for anything.

Not the way I *dressed*.

Or the way I *wore my hair*.

Or the way I *"talked like a White girl"*.

Or the music I listened to. We both could belt out a soulful rendition of Fantasia, get down with our "Buttermilk Biscuit", or "take over for the 9 9 and 2000", ya dig? Personally, my ear always leaned towards male mantras.

I sang with so much enthusiasm, one would think I had somehow managed the experiences of a man. What I didn't realize was much of what I was ingesting, musically, was shaping attitudes I would later internalize. Women were singing (and who didn't love a powerful voice?) but they just didn't seem in control. So many tears, so much heartache. It was like the woman *never* won. She always seemed to be accosted and somehow, ended up asking HIM back. There seemed to be no rationality, as though she didn't see what I saw. She'd be at home alone while her guy was out doing his thing…and she'd cry. It was strange. I couldn't ever understand why she just didn't leave. Seemed easy enough. I grew up never wanting to be "her". And "she" never fit me. I couldn't understand her thinking. Luckily, E and I were born only a few days a part in the same year, sharing astrological signs, creating a harmony between us that was unparalleled. Meaning, we shared many sentiments. She loved to sing and she, too, had been raised in a Christian home, so much of her music consisted of singers of all genres. We would warm up before games to samples of Ozzy Osbourne and she would hit the court, ready to take control of the floor. E was eventually able to parlay basketball into a D1 scholarship. Me, not so much. Seems I may have lacked the, uh, coordination and aggression to reach my maximum potential. It is what it is. I tried though. I tried reeeally hard. Coaches admired that. I'd started back in elementary school. My parents were very supportive, to say the least. Almost too supportive. And there were some things I merely wasn't good at, but I sojourned on. Between my long limbs that didn't fit until well into my high school years and those adorably thick lenses (complete with matching earstraps), my determination made for a long haul. I played all the way into my 17th year with a career filled with some of the most embarrassing times of my life. My shots spent more time in the bleachers than in the net. Once, I actually shot behind the goal. Sliding across gym floors in Payless sneakers must have brought some type of joy as a child because I always hustled harder after a long slide. That could have also been attributed to my wanting to prove that I was decent at at least one aspect of the game. One of the tallest girls on the court, and quite possibly one of the most gentle players you'd ever play, I never wanted to hurt anyone. Aggression just didn't befit me. In *any* way.

Empathy found home. Often, I found myself seeking to understand the heart of those that hurt me rather than being angry. Experiencing pain meant darkness, an incomparable darkness inside.

Digesting the motives and means for hurting one another created dissonance in my heart.

My music mirrored my sorrows, lamenting in my place when times called for fortitude. No one could know the secret that I bore.

Criticism, **hurt**.

Cynicism, **hurt**.

Malice, **hurt**.

Regardless of its direction, aim, or intended target, a fragment always found itself lodged in my heart. One aspect of life it took years to understand, to make peace with, was the gift of love. At the time, it presented more questions than answers as empathy seemed an overwhelming emotion.

When I was up, I was up. But when I was down, oh God, was I down. We all had our forms of rebellion, revolt; mine came in the form of woe.

--

Small Town, Alabama
2005.

It was a Sunday morning.

My mother sat at my bedside.

She asked me about something.

someone.

I told her I didn't know.

Aggravation set in at the ungrateful hour. Sundays were struggle enough, nobody even much felt for theatrics in the a.m.

He passed in a car accident last night.

Oh.

eyes still closed, it was as though her words somehow pierced the grey grog of fatigue. They echoed as she left the room.

spin.

I don't remember when I started crying or what year I stopped. Two gone, three forever changed.

Agony veiled over my shoulders, I roamed aimlessly about that first day, eyes brimming with tears that threatened escape at any moment. Still an indescribable feeling to this day, as even now, 10 years after, expressing how I felt is laborious. I'm not even sure the mind allows one to fully recall the depth of some pain. His death burdened me for years. Memories of our youthful flirtations flooded the days after, years after.

Obsessing days and nights, wondering had I been brave enough to tell him how I loved the smell of his hair, how I looked forward to his smile, what he'd thought in those final moments, if he ever even saw...

I'd never seen death before. His body lie still in a fashion that enforced the reality of his early, tragic departure. The boy I'd grown fond of lay before me, a stranger. His hair...wavy...pulled back. Perfect.

I had memories of him, lying there, still, for years. I would dream of him, see him at night all as I had seen him that final day.

There is no other word as clear and precise as pain.

--

She became my outcry. The only emotion I knew that was

safe to express. Misery was in her melody and her

company was welcome. She explained in, no uncertain

terms, the streaming from heart to brain and back again.

The thoughts. The ping-pong motion that crowded the

crevices of *control, its chaos was captured in her chords.*

As life escaped lungs, lost whispers sang sweet the adieus

of release. Feelings of failure complimented only by hot

tears were all to be managed in those final moments...

-

I'm sorry I wasn't enough

I'm sorry I couldn't do it

I'm sorry

I'm sorry...

Chapter 3

The roads wound endlessly, eyes glazed, salt sealed lips. Home grown, home gone and a familiar, yet new life lie ahead. Country commonalities settled me, but unrest was apparent. I'd found myself headed back to Oklahoma, bags in tow with my secret tucked away neatly inside. Like before, transfer was during a summer, presumably the best time to move a school-ager. Getting adjusted was a bit different this time though. Same city, except "home" was now my father's east side residence. I'd grown up with my mother on the west. All of the friends I had known were clear across town, but I was determined to make it work. Another new school and this time, I was prepared.

Social Media! *Brilliant idea.* I'd had a profile for some time, so it seemed like a great idea to find people in my new school to chat with online until the school year started. Now to be fair, this was during the initial big boom of the online networking era, so to me, this plan was foolproof and fairly harmless.

Sweet 16.

Those awkward limbs...not so awkward anymore (although I was the last one to get the memo). It was my 16th year and I had grown into a beautiful, chocolate doll; the problem was...*I* didn't know. Thin framed with jet black hair and fearless style, I once again found myself the center of unfavorable attention. Alabama had given me a break from the ridicule I'd suffered during my first year of junior high.

Although being skinny in the south was a feat of its own, it beat the taunting of my peers that'd came in the forms of cruel notes in my locker to jokes continuously made at my expense while I smiled in secret shame.

Sophomore year was a repeat of that familiar cycle. At certain ages, we are unable to comprehend the true meaning of abstract concepts such as love or friendship. Deeply, I yearned to be accepted so I'd allowed my "friends" to say things that unsettled me. I didn't want to be sensitive. They were only making jokes, right? Over the summer I'd gotten in touch with my two junior high buddies, one of which informed me that she had a boyfriend over at my new school who could show me around. I was eager for the help, so when he and I met for the first time, the comfort was immediate. Because we both shared a mutual love for my friend, (his love interest), we bonded immediately.

I officially had a friend, someone I knew would look out for me and help through this transition. To outsiders, however, it wouldn't look so innocent. Everyone knew he had a girlfriend, but no one on this side of town knew her or that she was my friend. Not to mention he was a star athlete who girls admired for his charm and uncanny similarities to the most famous pop singer at the time. After he began introducing me to his teammates, some of whom recognized me from my social media page, the next few weeks were a blur of confusion. Drama did not waste a moment in its arrival. As surely as I sauntered about that campus, corners were etched with conversation, the *whispered* kind that conveniently pauses when you walk by. And I noticed. When the attention from boys came, I *really* noticed. And for the life of me, I never knew what it was. Why me? Why would anyone notice *me*?

I was dark.

I was skinny.

Only enhanced by adornment, I'd accepted my fate long ago. Countless nights I'd spend dissecting my own reflection. The vision of myself bore such a shame that I could barely see through the tears. Faceless, smudged by loneliness, worthlessness. Unloved. *That* fate was the one I had come to terms with. It would always be that way. Yet, the adoration of male peers, especially, escaped me. No matter how badly I messed up, what I'd *done*, what they'd *heard*, they always had my back. The same could not be said of my female counterparts. A barrage of rumors, social media shenanigans, and gossip snowballed out of control. I found myself tumbling as wildly as the mill of tales. *She did WHAT?! With who?* I did?

On one end, I was livid. A fire had began to burn so feverishly inside of me, that I feared what would come if anyone ever got near its wrath. That anger, however, quickly dissipated into added pain. I was left to wonder what would drive a girl to hurt another, to actively seek out and destroy one another. The answer eluded me every time as I felt myself losing control. Sadness overwhelmed me in its grasp and I wasn't sure that I'd be able to hide it much longer. Rampantly running throughout times of rest, my mind would lie awake for hours contemplating the ways I could make it better.

I fell in love for the first time that year. By that, I mean to say I understood the abstract. I didn't realize it at the time, but this first, genuine act of commitment would be the catalyst for the start of a long healing process. He became my escape.

The years past of pain were expended in our hours of walking, talking, thinking. Countless nights under the stars we spent enjoying the Oklahoma winds. I was adjusting. I was still dealing with the loss of my friend along with the life that felt home to me shortly after, only to return...home? And start over? As though that weren't bludgeoning enough, I'd come with that *especially* guarded secret and its weight was becoming unbearable. At 16, I knew nothing but destruction. An ashen battlefield, my mind had no more energy to expend. I needed a breath of fresh air.

--

If you ever met him, he'd tell you this story himself. Our side of town was communal, especially the neighborhood.

Because we were made up primarily of military families, we shared that common bond. Watching our friends and families come and go was no occasion. Sad? Yes. But common. We all spent our days in school together, evenings in practice together, nights chatting and hanging out. One afternoon, I was two blocks up with the girls. We had drawn blocks on the ground to start a game of Four Square. I'd had my back to the street corner, so when the girls started whooping over the mysterious figure approaching, I followed suit. His body was amazing. Slender, just like I liked, and muscular. With the sun beaming down over his face and honey glazed skin, I was sure he was my next conquest. I had changed into a girl who knew what I wanted and made no bones about expressing it. He was getting closer. His walk carried such ease that it seemed a lifetime before we were able to place a name to the object of our shared affections.

Surely, he had a name. I mean, we knew everyone in the neighborhood...almost everyone in the school. Who *was* he? I squinted my eyes and leaned closer as I peered...

I knew him.

--smacks teeth-- "Man yall...that's just J."

And with a dismissive flick of the wrist, I returned to the game and the girls followed suit.

He and I spent two years after that tutoring each other. I was horrendous at math and he...well...let's just say writing this book wouldn't have been on his list of things to do. We both had honors classes, so failing was not really an option. Hours a day, he spent coaching me through math. He had flattered himself to think I was doing all of that to gain more of his time.

I was not, but it definitely was a perk. But his English skills weren't any better. Now...this next portion of the story is not intended to encourage young women to repeat this behavior. Had I had the sense God gave a goose, I would have let his butt be. Fate didn't have that in the cards though. The same boy I had ridiculed on the street that day became the only person I saw. In those hours we'd spent bumbling through poems and otherwise destroying the metric system as we know it, I learned of his love of basketball and peanut butter cups. His scent became familiar to me as I would ease closely to him just to steal a whiff. His slang became my amusement as I sat alone in my room at night listening to how his phrases sounded from my lips. I always felt cooler when I used his words. He was cool. Everybody loved J. He was a Jr., hence the nickname. Star athlete, stellar student, all the guys were his friends and all the girls were too, even though most were secretly dying to be more. He was the nice guy, the one who always listened when you were having problems with your boyfriend. He was funny and every girl loved his particular take on the truth, often dry and perceived as sarcasm but adored, nonetheless; and, here I was, loving him. And he did not love me back. He actually had only intended to be a friend to me. I found myself opening up to him. Sometimes my secret was too much to bear, wholly. In him I found my sounding board, unloading my thoughts on the one person who'd actually worked for my trust. We had sat at the neighborhood park one darkening afternoon. I wanted him to meet me there after a particularly hard day of trying to stay focused in class and the latest high school headlines.

Yet again, I was the talk of the school. Another rumor spread due to particular male affiliations.

Why did they care so much? I couldn't understand it. I walked to the park that day, secret stuffed away, because today, I was ready. Colorful, beaded bracelets hid the only visible trace of my past. I needed to talk to someone. The pressure of all the things I'd been holding inside was becoming agonizing. Nights had reduced my being to pools of tears and days weren't much clearer. Often times, I would catch myself gasping for air, doing all I could to hold on. I was at my breaking point. That was evident to my classmates, some of which seized the opportunity to let me know how worthless I was. Comments urging suicide were left on my social media pages. The world had become tizzy of death, depression, and rain. Vision only allowed for the three.

Befitting, that it'd be a gloomy day. A calm rested over me as I made the decision to trust him with my secret. We sat atop the jungle gym as I finally came clean. I opened up my heart to him revealing insecurities I'd hidden from myself, even.

Sweet tears of surrender streamed from my eyes and he caught every one. I'd never felt much safer than I did in that moment. He didn't judge me like so many others had. He listened. As I cried, I began to explain how I'd never felt loved, how hard it was to accept attempts of love because of its showings in the past. I told him how sick I felt inside, how broken and alone I was after returning to Oklahoma. He felt my heart. His arms came and went as times called for silence, some for laughter. He, too, opened up to me, not necessarily with his own experiences, but he allowed himself to absorb mine.

As I cried, head down in shame, I finally unpacked the secret I had brought with me. I sat before him and shared the story of my moving back to Oklahoma, how I'd tried to end my own life and the despair that led up to it. For once, I could breathe again. Letting someone in had been so hard. We parted ways as the storm began to clear. The rain gave way to a rainbow, the only sign of hope I had that maybe all would be well.

I spent some of the best moments of my teenage years with J. Quite candidly; I'd spent my sophomore and junior year chasing him down. Yes, he'd told me he wasn't interested in a relationship. That's fine. He only said that because he hadn't been in a relationship with *me.* See the difference there? All it would take was for him to see I wasn't like everyone else. I wasn't who they said I was. Someone had to know that. Someone had to believe me.

He did. My infatuation was the product of energies stored from my past.

I'd fallen into an isolation that harbored an unspeakable despair, along the way, learning to hide those aspects of mine that didn't quite fit the norm. A shell of myself, I had been rejected so much for being "weird", I was afraid no one would ever accept me. All those years of begging God's grace from my own hand, I just needed a friend. J was that. We laughed together incessantly. It was the first and last time I was able to express my affection, my full spectrum of emotion, without fear of reproach. Beauty assumed a new ideal. The world was our kingdom. Each day was a chance to try something new, to experience life in all of its boldness and stretch the idea of limitations. Selflessness never meant sacrifice because my happiness lie in his.

When he finally decided to make me his girlfriend, it was nearing the time of our senior prom. His tonsils had been an issue, so the decision was agreed upon to remove them. I'd taken on the responsibility of caring for him. Although his mother wasn't the most avid fan of our budding romance, she didn't mind the help or company for her son. At the time, I was working, full time, at a hotel on the nearby military base. The job paid well and the people I worked with were colorful. People from across the globe were my fancy: Russia, Croatia, Romania, Czech Republic. I'd made a practice of keeping my work uniform in the car because my shift was always immediately after school.

The afternoon after his surgery, I'd text him, letting him know I was going to work for my usual 3-11. What I discovered upon my arrival was that a housekeeper had missed her shift.

I was asked to tidy up a few rooms for arrivals in exchange for leaving when I finished and a full shift's pay. One would assume the prospect of an early departure from my job with no penalty, in itself, would have been the primary benefit in the situation. No; It was being able to surprise J as one of the first visitors at home after his surgery. He'd be so happy to see me. It'd become common knowledge among our classmates that he and I were "talking", meaning involved with each other in some form. No one knew the exact manner. For us (once I finally got my emotions together), there was a thrill in existing in our own world. We had grown to see the beauty in our predicament. I arrived at his house to the sight of two cars parked along the curb. Guess I wasn't the first to get there. Upon entering, I briefly spoke to his mother who informed me he was resting in the back. As I rounded the corner, I could hear the voices of girls in his room. Only two. Both familiar. My steps began to slow and then falter as I contemplated leaving. I still wasn't his girlfriend after two years and the lengths to which his female admirers would go for his attention was getting old. With no proper title, however, I was limited on what I could address with the ladies and every time I spoke with him about it, he assured me that it didn't mean anything to him.

"There could be all the girls in the world in the stands and after the game, I'll still be looking for you. Well...unless Gabrielle Union was in the stands..."

Had to love his honesty.

"Suck it up and go see him," I said to myself.

Wouldn't you know I walked into the room and one of the girls laid up in his bed, big, round behind pressed up against him while the other stood frozen stock still.

Apparently, *everyone* had expected me to be at work. That's what I get for surprising people.

I smiled sweetly, mouth tight as she crept out of his bed in slight embarrassment. There wasn't much to say after that, so she and her friend suddenly found some place else to be. I wheeled around and turned my attention to him. All the while, he'd been wearing his killer smile and basketball shorts. Handsome, as usual, he began to flash that smile my way and beckon me closer so that he could enjoy his surprise visitor. I was upset and wasted no time in letting him know. He didn't care. He simply pulled out his dry erase board his mother had given him to communicate and began to explain. His throat was still sore, so this would have to do. Turns out, I hadn't been the only one who'd shown up unexpectedly. The two girls had also come as a surprise.

"Oh! You're just full of surprises today" I remarked tossing my hands in the air.

We laughed as I fell back into his arms and began to breathe the air surrounding his space. We carried on a conversation that way, him wrapped around me with the white board to respond to questions I asked aloud. As he updated me on his progress and how great he was feeling despite not being able to talk, I lost myself in his love. Over the past two years, our relationship had grown from non-existent, to tutors, to my slight fatal attraction phase, to developing a true friendship, to what felt like love sweltering around us. It was March and senior prom was one month away. It'd been on my mind to remind him. We hadn't quite confirmed if *we* were going together or not. Or..if we were together. Or exactly what we were doing.

"Baby, I was thinking…" as I turned toward him.

Before I could finish, he motioned to the dry erase board.

"Will you be my girlfriend?"

Chapter 4

Choosing a college had been particularly difficult for a number of reasons. First, I'd always been of the mind that if one simply goes to school and performs well, division one scholarships would practically find you! Negative. Definitely not the case. I had always pictured myself becoming an English teacher.

As high school winded down I was overwhelmed with the college admission process. Not only had I not fully been aware of the avenues to attain scholarships, I had no idea about the application fees! Here I was, a high school senior working a job at a military lodging facility, trying to go on to college and I had no help. My GPA had been great. I was able to graduate with a 4.33, but it wasn't enough.

Class rankings showed that some of my classmates would, in fact, graduate with 5.0 averages not to mention their slew of credentials, accolades, and involvements.

Once I figured out my pocketbook was not going to allow my fairytale dorm days to be, I had to get real. J and I had discussed our collegiate plans many a night and it had always looked like he would be in-state on an athletic scholarship and I would be off at some massive campus on the east coast. Neither of us, though, had really considered the possibility of going to college together. It wasn't a bad idea. Our relationship had always been comfortable. We were friends who fell in love.

Once we made it official a few months back I'd seen an improvement.

He was no longer hesitant or unsure of his love for me. At school, people often pulled him aside to ask him if he "knew [D] has been going around telling people she's your girlfriend". He would always smile.

"She is."

I left for school before he did. June 2009. A few days after Mike died.

There was nothing left for me in town. After we'd announced our relationship, I'd grown aware of the extent of secret jealousies. I was only invited to the "cool" parties because I was his girlfriend and sometimes that still didn't warrant an invitation. I must admit, I did sit at home alone on occasion while he would go out with his friends. It wasn't his fault I wasn't invited. Why should I hinder him from the privileges afforded by "popular". See, I was a different kind of popular.

The kind of girl everyone speculated about, told stories of, but never really knew; almost like an urban legend.

They never knew what *she* liked, never gave her a birthday dinner, seems like she had a lot of friends though. It'd *always* seemed like I had lots of friends. Either way, I only felt the weight of my social leprosy when I couldn't have him by my side. He loved me, flaws and all.

So when it came time for me to go, I left quietly, enlisting only the aid of my father, my boyfriend and three of our close friends. The idea of putting together forced facades, parties that mayn't have come together at all, exhausted me. Yes, I feared no one would show for me. The friendships I had formed and maintained throughout my time there few.

I'd saved myself the disappointment and headache, choosing an average day in the early morning to set off into my new life of adulthood and independence. I had scouted the town where my boyfriend and I would start our new life.

A small, one bedroom apartment in walking distance from his dorms is what I chose. No, we did not live together and made no plans to do so. Just being in close proximity was enough for us. Although we had been together for what already felt like years, we both understood the importance of space and enjoyed our own.

Regardless of our spending every single day together, there was still a special quality of having the option to separate but choosing to spend so much time with each other. My freshman year in college was when I discovered my love for traveling and autonomy.

It felt as though I was living life the "right" way. You go to school. You graduate. You move out, go to college, and start your own life and that is precisely what I did. I found work at a local bar and such was the beginning of my college years.

Classes were easy, but nothing was the same. Being on campus somehow felt hollow. Yes, the routine should have been easier. I should have been happy right? I had my own apartment, my own space to do things how I wanted and, I mean, I'd been going to class my entire life, so what was so different now? Why had the task gotten so difficult and intolerable?

Being on my own came with a slew of challenges I had not anticipated, especially financially. Initially, I had help with my rent and was able to budget and manage with the gig I had.

I worked late into the nights as students and locals came together singing the "Sweet Caroline" at each night's end.

BUM. BUM. BUM.

The bar was great. I had no complaints. I loved my little life. I came home every night from work, late, but rarely alone. J had a key. After long practices, sometimes he'd want to get away and have a private shower outside of the communal in the dorms. I usually cooked before I left, anticipating him. Most times, he was already in my queen size bed, asleep, mouth wide with *Top 10* streaming highlights in the background.

Our mutual circle of high school friends had also gone to colleges in the state. We traveled together on weekends to party with them. Some weekends we would go together. Others he'd stay in town while I would head to the city for a girl's night out.

He and I spent Sundays traveling back and getting ready for the week; studying, resting, and at the library. We enjoyed our little life of routine and togetherness and all was well until one odd day at my job.

Business was unusually slow. To me, there was really no cause for concern because of the constant fluctuation of college towns. The managers tended to agree, as newer employees began to express their concerns. The older servers and I chalked it up to a dry spell and continued mulling about in our usual mundane enthusiasm. However, what we thought was an isolated incident turned out to be a major problem. Our business was one impacted by the recession. When the economy began to waver, people just weren't eating out as much. Even college students were a bit tighter with their financial aid refunds.

The bar was locally owned and only had one other location, by no means a franchise. Steadily, business declined until we were forced to shut our doors, leaving me with no job and rent, electricity, gas, and credit card bills (from all of those college application fees and deposits) to pay.

J was there for moral support, but unfortunately that was all he was able to give. Because he was on an athletic scholarship, his schedule afforded him very little free time, certainly not enough to get a job and help me out. When I was finally able to find work almost two months later, I was so far behind in bills that I ensued in a game of catch up, maxing out hours at work to try and get stable. School was very important, of course, but what was school if I had no place to sleep at night or no food to eat?

Working around the clock to meet my costs of living, I wasn't able to focus on school for weeks on end. The college life was not what I had pictured. I was no stranger to hard work, but between trying to get my expenses situated and give effort to class the pressure was on. I made the choice to devote more time to work, causing my grades to drop and my attendance to decrease. Each semester, I was caught between wanting to lead the life I'd seen on TV and trying to maintain a home by myself. The routine of college fatigued me and I was consumed with trying to stay afloat. I started to sink deeply into myself. I was drifting further from the few friends I had. Some left school, choosing different paths while others, I simply stopped calling.

--

Peace was there. She was an Aries so the bounds of her affection...well, there were none. Our conversations began in one of our many shared English courses, discussing our disapproval of the politics of higher education, namely the grading system and tedious assignments masked as general requirements. We started spending time together, often choosing other ways to spend beautiful days than sitting in a classroom of a stuffy classroom.

Our differences allowed us both to more intimately explore life. Peace was from a different south. She was raised in a small, conservative town in Texas, predominately White.

She stood out. The way she dressed, the freedom, no matter where she went, people noticed her, much like I had. However, whereas most people just noticed, we connected. She became my ally. We spoke the language of debate and knowledge perusing subjects from the pointless rhetoric of predesigned courses as opposed to a path of coursework suitable for each individual to the misrepresentation of minorities in the media. I began to explore my own freedoms in the confines of our world. I'd made a friend. The burdens of poverty and depression seemed lighter as I learned to bear its weight in my poetry. That same year, I had taken a creative writing course. I was ecstatic, reading the course title over and over again. This is what I was in school for: the broadening of my knowledge in literary techniques and discussing The Greats. Definitely not what happened. I'd again been the only Black person in the class which meant two things: I was immediately the spokesperson for Black people nationwide and no one understood my work. Critiques on Peer Day always flew in, muddled with red penned question marks. My discouragement became evident throughout the course. In addition to my money woes, it was no wonder I woke feeling weary most days.

However, this specific day had been unusual. I woke feeling outside of myself. I couldn't it. All day, I moved about in a gray film of sullen emotion unable to accurately what I was feeling. I'd told my classmate, Underwood, something was wrong.

She and I had, like me and Peace, developed a bond through the classes we all shared although, admittedly, she was a much more responsible student than the two of us.

She watched over me with a nurturing protection. I called her Auntie. Her energy was always pleasant, long before I'd known of its power. I had been comfortable enough with her to confess to her my struggles with depression and less than enthused disposition towards attendance policies. She understood and was there.

Willing myself up the stairs of the Language Arts building, Auntie was waiting inside. We walked to Creative Writing that day. I showed her my latest work.

Drowning...

The air closed tightly around lungs collapsed, crushed waves.

Crushed waves herald the story of the drowning girl.

For she never had a chance in it.

Love it is,

Breath of fresh

Water filled lungs.

Drowning...

Auntie looked at me inquisitively. Her mind raced to process the root of this unfamiliar mood. Displacement was the consensus as we both walked into the classroom that day unsure of what we felt, but we'd both agreed, something was wrong.

Reading that poem aloud gave me the clarity that had been absent all day. It was J. He had been with someone else. I knew who she was. Months ago, I'd warned him of the sort of conversation he kept with her after she'd text him one evening. J was in the shower after an especially difficult practice. He asked me to respond to a text message alert on his phone.

Walking into the bedroom to get it, I noticed it was the name of a girl from our hometown. I'd known she was interested, to say the least.

She was a family friend of his who had been a problem to our relationship since its start.

I read the message out to him, his forearm extended above the shower rod as he washed. Her tone had been so deliberate, words strategic. The texting wasn't new information to me. I knew they talked. I trusted J. Seeing her number was no shock to me, especially since he had made it clear that she was like part of the family. I gently warned him of the impeding trouble as he washed away my concern with the day's workout.

When I discovered the news, it was though I'd already known. A dull ache had been present in my heart before he had ever said a word. Emptiness began to creep back inside of me, reclaiming its former home.

Although, I had predicted the outcome of their exchanges, it did little to soften the blow. Haloed street lights while driving city streets was the scene for many nights as I struggled to process it all. Digging deep into my senses I searched myself for answers. Yes, I was upset. I was hurt. But I'd known from the moment he confessed that I wasn't going anywhere. I believe I'd made that decision months before when I'd suspected the possibility. Candidly, there is an element in the realization that your superman isn't perfect that really changes the way you see life. Throughout our love I'd learned so much. He'd given me the ability to see myself a bit more clearly and that there was more to me to love than what met the eye. I learned to accept. I accepted him for who he was. I accepted the responsibility of loving him. For me, that meant acknowledging his faults and deciding internally, what I was willing to deal with, what

I was willing to take.

With broken forgiveness, I put my bid in to make it work. As time would have it, I would need him after a failed roommate situation threatened the sliver of stability I'd gained. The upside was I would be able to have my own space again, also giving J and I the space we needed to work on our relationship. In my 20th year, I, again, was starting over. Fourth apartment and a another of issues to work through with the man I loved. My path had tightened its ever winding coils, as I wondered how I would face it all. I barely had the money to get a new place, much less possess the strength to trying to rebuild my relationship with him. We committed to it, though. I committed to trying to fix it all, make it work. From school to money and J in between, I committed to getting myself out of this mess. At what cost was the only true question. How much was I willing to take?

Chapter 5

The fallout from the past year's events had become intense. The gas station I had been working at hired a slew of new employees and opened a new store, therefore, reducing my hours and exacerbating my already strained wallet. I had become a prisoner to my own thoughts, often not left with much else. My new apartment required a drive, so J hadn't been over nearly as much and I kind of liked it that way. Not because I didn't want to see him. Not at all. It's just… the shame I felt about my final financial situation was so great that I couldn't even open up to my best friend. Less than a year ago, he'd kicked himself from the pedestal I held him on. human. I forgot for a moment.

Between me and you, Reader, I never thought he was perfect.

It's just, you know what the person you love will and won't do. Deep down, we know who they are and we choose whether or not we will accept that. And if we are *especially in sync*, we know the nature of their heart. I knew his heart. The aching I'd felt in mine was his. The poem I'd written, I later found, was only days after his indiscretion. That's how in tune we were. I was not willing to give up what we built for a mistake. But it broke my heart. J had broken my heart and we had to start over. Our foundation had kept us grounded, but the fortress couldn't be rebuilt, at least not the same way.

My situation came to a head when my thinning income forced choices between necessities. Rent or electricity during a record setting winter was a monthly quandary.

There was no feeling worse than coming home from class to a cold house, not having time to digest it all because you've still got to get ready for work. And even work did not seem to be working out. I was making enough to cover most of my expenses, but not all of them. On my way up the stairs to my apartment one afternoon after class, I noticed a note on the door. As I neared the entrance, I'd dropped my book bag spilling its content onto the landing. "Great," I thought to myself. I was exhausted. Gathering the rest of my supplies, I ripped the taped note from the door and let myself inside. My living room was set up just so. Two black rocking chairs with rocking footstools, a blue striped couch, and a TV. I plopped down on the sofa and hit the power button on the remote. Nothing. I grabbed the note and pulled apart the tape that held its poles together.

EVICTION NOTICE.

There it was as clear as day. I stared at that paper as though all of my hard work lie in its contents. I saw traces of my time at school play back in my mind. The reality set in that I was about to lose my apartment. That night, I lay in my bed alone, and cried the loneliest cry my heart had ever known. I felt hopeless. Here I was again, in a bind I couldn't get myself out of with no one to turn to. My diet had been reduced to warm soda to fill the empty space in my stomach when cabinets went bare. Sometimes I was able to save up enough money to buy a 5 dollar cheese stick box, my guilty pleasure, providing an escape from the pressures of life. But I was getting sick. The constant battle to maintain an apartment had worn me down mentally and physically. I was tired of fighting. I had nothing left to give, not to school, not to J, not to responsibilities. Empty. There was no money for food. The pain of hunger had become so common that I had to learn how to mentally will myself through it. There was class and work and studying: things that needed to be done. The best chance of that getting accomplished was for me to learn how to survive. I was never certain of my next meal, allowing my fear and shame to separate me from the outside world. I mean, who could I tell? No one was going through problems like this. And it seemed like, even when I mentioned small instances that bothered me, my friends would expect me to "be strong". It was as though I didn't show enough emotion for anyone to take me seriously. It wasn't that I wasn't hurt. On the contrary, I was shattered inside. Each day had become a choice for me. Some days I just wanted to lay down and die. Everything I once enjoyed became distant memories while I encouraged J to go out more with *his* friends. It gave me more time to be alone. To think. I didn't want him around me while I dealt. I was sinking further into a depression that left me feeling as though I was literally spiraling downward. Tears flowed down my face nightly as I wondered how I would make it through school. I couldn't afford to stay there. I couldn't even afford to buy a decent winter coat to walk to class in. I'd have to sneak into the dorms with J some nights because my electricity would be turned off. This particular evening though, I'd chosen to be cold. I chose to lie in my cold apartment, with no electricity buried underneath a fleece blanket and a comforter a top my bed. The humiliation I felt developed into disappointment. School had been a nightmare for me. Progressive anxiety kept me from the inside of the actual classroom as if the other students could see the words "POOR" and "BROKEN" written clearly across my forehead. I couldn't even manage to take care of myself. My shoes were coming apart at the soles, and it weren't for J I wouldn't have even had a warm place to lay my head some nights. Well, my car of course. But going back home wasn't an option. I had given up too much. What did home even mean? Was that what was meant for the people you loved, who loved you? Thinking about the years, I thought back to all of the people who'd told me they loved me, cared for me. Where were they? I lay curled in my own defeat. Deafening, blackened silence surrounded me. My mind split into two distinctive voices, choices. The secret that I thought I had let go so long ago in the park with J, haunted me. It sat perched upon my shoulder as I gasped helplessly for air. That drowning sensation had again seized me. I cried out in mental agony. I sat engulfed in the excrement of pain, head hung between sullen shoulders. The pressure welled inside my chest as though I were on the verge of exploding. There was no release. The agony had dug itself too deep. I stumbled hazily into my living room to find anything to relieve the pain. A flashlight to guide, I found a bottle of prescription cough syrup lying on the floor. Quietly and alone, I sipped beneath my covers until the pain was gone...

--

Depression had become a part of my life again, creeping its way in through a moment of weakness. Better days came, but not without its imprint, the sadness. I found a job that paid a bit more than the one before and I had worked especially hard to move into my next space, a townhouse across the street from J's dorm, just a walk across the parking lot. He and I had gone through a tough winter. Seeing me in such a weakened state really tested our relationship. Watching me struggle to hold on really tore him apart.

I often tried to grasp for the words to let my baby know it wasn't his fault. And he heard me, but it didn't stop the pain, the helplessness of knowing there was nothing he could do for me.

Seeing me suffer was hard for him to bear at times, but he stayed. With the aid of his love, I was able to give myself a fighting chance. The language of silent battles came with a resilience, as though I'd been sent here for something and I had to know what that was. Too many times, I'd faced death. Too many. Yet, I stood, battered, but standing. I needed to know why.

My new home, a one bedroom townhouse, was an accomplishment. Work had come steady enough to afford it and begin taking care of other expenses. I even had money to enjoy things I loved. There was a restaurant off of Route 66 that had the best lemon pepper tilapia. My usual waitress always remembered my order.

She treated me with such respect. I always tipped as much as I could and even on days I couldn't she was always grateful. Peace and I would go there to indulge in the finer things, in our own small town kind of way.

My relationship had really turned around, too. J even bought me a promise ring, a token of our undying friendship to one another. Things felt like they did at the very beginning of our relationship, almost. But could we really expect it all to be the same. We were older now. J was no longer playing football and concentrating more on school and his career. And I, I was just there. I was working and going to school, but that was all. I was not any more happy there than I had been before. The only benefit was my new location. I loved my home, but even it had felt like a hollow victory.

I took my first spring break trip that year.

Peace and I along with two other of our friends decided to take a trip to South Padre Island.

J and I decided to take separate trips that year which was rare because we went everywhere together, even places that our friends didn't think a relationship could last in, clubs, bars, parties.

One year, J and I went to a hotel party. It was the first of its kind in the state. It featured rooms that overlooked the lobby for those guest who could afford to spend more. We made a reservation and drove up to the city that weekend. That had to be the best party we ever went to together. See, we'd always been secure in what we had, so if we went out there was no room for jealousy. He danced with other girls. I danced with other guys. And by the end of the night like clockwork, we always ended up on the dance floor together, swapping stories of the people we met and how our moves held up.

I was definitely the better dancer. This time, though, there would be no cute two steps from the "happy couple". The ride home from Padre was quiet congested only with the sound of heavy traffic and bad decisions. I'd told the girls about our last night in paradise and the decision I'd made. Peace was the first to know. I woke up the next morning with an intense unease in my belly. She got up when I left the bed to wash my face. We walked down to the pool, where I told her about the enigmatic man I'd been weak with. He'd filled a void that lay empty for months. You have to understand, when someone you love slips into a depression it's very hard for their partner to understand that they are not the cause. J had taken distance in my darkest hour. The isolation I felt from the outside world was the same he felt from me. So in months prior it'd been the

Do you still love me?

Am I beautiful to you?

Why do you seem so distant…

My self-esteem had faltered wondering why my baby was not present when I came home from my mental hiatus. I had to go away. I had to save myself, so I could be better for him, for me. But upon my return I faced the ashen flames in his eyes. The kid I'd tumbled into love with my sophomore year in high school was slowly fading away before my eyes. It was as though I'd caught him on the way out of the door. We'd always discussed marriage. Yet, after almost six years in each other's lives, neither of us were ready to get married. We weren't ready to move in together. And it was ok. We were fine with where we were. But why? I pondered, looking back over the time we'd spent together. Family drama, holidays apart because his mother, who had once loved me, no longer wanted me around.

Long practices. Degree decisions. Hospital trips where one had been too sick to fill in medical information. Sulfa drugs. He was allergic to Sulfa drugs. I always knew to tell the doctors that when he was too ill to speak for himself. We fought through it all; my past of self-harm, abuse, and isolation, naysayers and people who had tried to take us from one another and here I was, questioning us. But Padre had been proof that something was wrong with us. Telling him the next day, I felt numb as I watched the hurt flicker in his eyes, replaced by responsibility. He had always felt the day would come when I would take karma into my own hands. That hadn't been the case, but he believed it and accepted my mistake that way, agreeing to move on. Peace and I spent the better portion of that summer together. Our conversations had changed from the latest university gossip to more about the constraints societal norms, indie music, and abstract art.

We even started painting! I didn't know what was going on inside of me.

It was like, I wasn't interested in the same things anymore. As far as school, it just wasn't for me. I realized that. But I was going to finish, because I started and I was almost done with one year left. A tiny shift had occurred within me. I still was uneasy about the spring break incident even though it had been months ago. I still couldn't figure out what I had done it.

Explorations. Truly searching for the answer to my questions led me to find more than I'd intended. I finally realized…I had no idea who I was. I had no identity outside of J. I was J's girlfriend or Peace's friend. But never just… D.

Seems I'd always preferred it that way, maneuvering from E's shadow in Alabama, into sharing the light with J and Peace. But never *just* D. Who was I?

What did I like? What did I even want to do with my life? School was still a hassle, draining every ounce of energy and money I had. Why was I even *here*? Because of him. He'd always selflessly asked over the years had I considered transferring schools. He could see that I wasn't happy there, but I stayed. He was all I needed. Plus, I couldn't leave him alone. Who would take care of him when he was sick? Proofread his papers, cook him dinner after long practice nights, show up at his games to encourage him through his waning interest in football. Through our relationship, he had learned to open up about his deepest fears and insecurities, a feat, I learned, was not easy for any man. He confided in me. He loved me. For the first time in his life, he *truly* loved. How could I even consider leaving him?

And yet, as quickly as I'd answered one question came another, and another. What did I want? Where would I go? If I left, how would I live without him? It occurred to me that he had become my crutch over the years. I did need him. We'd coached each other through the hardest moments in both of our lives. Our relationship sustained fire from almost every person that mattered in our lives. We lost friends and strained dealings with our own families for each other. But neither one of us would let go; we'd needed each other.

As I stood alone in the driveway of my townhome that starry evening, the words floated down from the skies on the whispered winds of the universe.

"If you love him, let him go."

no. No. Let him go? What do you mean let him go?

I made the hardest decision of my life that night. The heat in the bottom of my stomach rose throughout my chest and spread to my back, rolled over my shoulders, and into my throat as I waited for him to pick up the phone. We stayed on the phone for 25 minutes exactly. Muted lips motioned the words I'd rehearsed. The truths I'd discovered.

drowning.

Tell me nothing has changed.

"Baby, tell me nothing has changed. I'll stay. I promise

I'll stay…"

Silence.

Coveted moments we spent listening through each other. The silence sweetened its tone as we sat wondering if there was more to be said that warm July night. He was home with his family and I, well I too was at home.

The last of our conversation was spent reminiscing on days gone by and him giving me his final blessing to relocate. Reluctantly, we let each other go, but not without spending one last night with each other. We lay on separate couches, backs turned, in our separate emotions. I knew he was hurt, and so was I, but we both knew it had to be done. Unspoken unrest settled in as the heat drifted through an open window. I felt a gentle hand come to rest on my back. As I rolled over into his arms, he picked me up off the couch, tears in his eyes. And we danced. One last time. Frank Ocean, soft, in the summer night's breeze.

Chapter 6

The summer of my 21st year led me to Texas.
Heat sweltered high as emotions inside my Altima.
Everything I'd known was left behind in the dusty back
roads of Oklahoma. I suppose it'd become a habit,
picking up and leaving. The air was thicker there.
Probably the humidity. Or maybe even my own
excitements and anxieties clouded the atmosphere.
However, housed in another small town, my new campus
was absolutely beautiful. I'd rode around with an
elementary school friend of mine who had agreed to be
my roommate. Before I left Oklahoma, I'd called her,
only citing that I needed a change of scenery.

When she found out J and I hadbroken up (because, of course, we all went to high school together) she was shocked, much like everyone else who'd known us as a unit. We were either our cities most beloved couple or its most infamous, but either way everyone had taken their bets. Seems I'd lost.

That July, she and I moved into a two bedroom townhome, shamelessly spending our days and nights creeping for the most sought after men on campus via social media. Our own apartment complex was one of the hang out spots; cars ceaselessly parading in and out, music blaring. Summer parties were our chance to get out of the house and away from our usual late night walks around the buildings in our slippers. Absently, I'd forgotten about the "new girl syndrome" that seemed to follow everywhere I went. But the attractions were almost undeniable here.

I felt the stares of unfamiliars everywhere I went.

The first time I was approached was after a party at one of the frat houses. I found myself talking to a handsome, young man with a slow, southern accent. We spoke in brief as he walked me to my car. The way I was dressed left me wondering if he'd made a mistake. I wore a long purple sundress and sandals while the other girl's clothes were hanging on for dear life. He opened the car door for me, bidding good night, and leaving behind only the sultry scent of his cologne. As he slowly walked away it occurred to me that I was no longer the young girl I'd been when I started dating J years ago. These were men and the stakes weren't the same out here in Texas.

Not entirely different though. As soon as I'd first stepped foot onto campus, the rumors began to fly, especially after I was seen talking to the young man from the party that night on more than one occasion and remembered from a few summertime kickbacks.

I felt changed.

My freedom had allowed me a confidence that didn't care as much to entertain the musings of others. Their thoughts on my life weren't my problem, so as far as I was concerned, I was going to continue allowing them to believe whatever they wanted without so much as a wrinkle in my poker face.

School added a new dynamic for me. After elementary school I had always attended diverse schools or PWIs altogether. Although this was listed as the same, the student center was filled with brown faces. Every day I watched Black students of different backgrounds and upbringings interact with each other. The fashion, impeccable style, and love of their city bonded so many together. It was that bond, along with relentless ambition, that propelled some of those students into the highest ranking offices of organizations, campus wide. I was floored. Never had I seen, firsthand, young, Black leaders. Designated days marked the dedication to class and refinement as members of these orgs dressed in their best, and I do mean their best, business attire.

It was then that I discovered my weakness for men in tailored suits.

The ladies weren't much further behind. I'd seen some bags, shoes, and hair, but NEVER anything like this; college girls with outfits that priced well into the hundreds and Brazilians to match. As much as I enjoyed the environment, I had other things to worry about. Transferring so hastily had caused more problems than one. Financially, it'd set me back. I maxed out the two credit cards I had between moving vans, admission fees, and deposits. I had also lost a substantial amount of credit hours to the switch equating to a semester and a half. It was heartbreaking, but the choice I'd made wasn't up for debate.

The weight of my new environment began to bear down on me heavily. Classes had only been in session two months and I'd already come to a few conclusions. Number one, no matter where I went, school just didn't seem to be the move.

Yet again, I found myself drudgingly getting to classes. Depression often lingered in the mornings as I forced myself to put some effort into all of the money I had spent trying to attain this degree...which meant absolutely nothing to me. Number two, As much as I loved the tradeoff of this university over the other I'd attended, my new school mates had been intently watching and everything from what I wore to who I held conversation with was cause for discussion. It all seemed so trivial to me. Being with J had shielded me from the antics of outsiders for many years. Yes, people had much to say of us, but it never mattered to him, therefore, it never mattered to me. I had always been spoken of, but I thought college would be an exception. I believed that everyone would be so enthralled in their own dealings that a regular girl like me would go largely unnoticed minus the few who chose to partake in my peculiar company. I was stumped. This experience needed to be manageable. I enlisted the aid of a friend I'd made there. In those short months, Renita had been my right hand. I had never met anyone who accepted me fully and without judgment. It was though we'd known each other for years. We spoke about J as though she had been present for the duration of our relationship. She became my guardian angel and because she had been at this university longer than I, her ear was a bit closer to the street. And it worked well that way. Searching for answers was but a piece of the journey, a piece I hadn't the time to focus on. I wanted to be single. I wanted to be D. Not D and… _____ or D and… _____ Just me. I lived the life I wanted and Renita respected me for it. As long as I was happy, she was happy for me.

At length, we discussed my concerns.

"School isn't for everyone", she said.

It wasn't the first time I'd heard the mantra; it was just the first time I believed it. Even though I had lost an incredulous amount of hours, I was determined to finish. Why? Because I didn't have a choice. Where would I go? What else would I do? How would I get a decent job? I'd already invested so much time. Why not just finish, right? Except my grades were plummeting and my professors had no kind words for my unique writing style. Essay after essay, my aim was at least get a letter grade of C. If I could at least do that, I could pass. Even though this campus had a larger African American population, I suppose there weren't many Black students interested in teaching high school English, which made it harder for me and the other two of us to express opinions that conflicted with some already delicate psyches.

That said, I was never in a rush to head to class and play devil's advocate especially during racially charged literary reviews. I hadn't the time, the energy, nor the patience for the narrow-minded, ignorant, comments that often came with the discussion of literature, especially of southern descent.

Renita and I sat inside of her silver four door sedan staring aimlessly into the distance. I thought back to my arrival here. So much was new about this place. Surely I could find an adventure to embark on that made this feel worthwhile.

And then there was a lightbulb.

Organizations! That was it. It'd be a new experience, potentially one that could motivate me to graduate. I had never been in an org before, not even in high school, and had not the faintest clue what they were really about.

What I did know was that there was a void in my life that I wanted to fill. I wanted to belong. Be a part of something greater than myself, perhaps in hopes of losing myself in it. Being the outsider had grown tiring while everything inside of me yearned to just be normal. I wanted to have friends too. I wanted to hang out at The Spot too. Having seen other Black students excelling in their respective orgs allowed for the idea that I could, too, be a part of something and be somebody, if I so chose to be. So I applied.

Now, regarding the petty of my population, well, it was nothing new. But for some reason, it bothered me every time because it happened everywhere I went. I could just never understand *why.*

Why is this still happening?

Why would anyone be so invested in me?

I'm weird, right? And for you, weird means abnormal.

Strange. Undesirable.

--

Conflicted feelings flooded fears of being without you.

My whole life had become an ode to your greatness.

Boxes filled with memories, remember he? I remembered

me. But she, was no more. Where was her beginning?

For we had seen her untimely end. Yet her end was her

begin. And through the rose colored lens, her luster

shone from within. But she was blind. She could not,

would not see. Bound by lies of which they told,

convincing her she was nothing special to behold but, Oh

Queen. Dear Queen...

I hadn't done a pageant since the year 19 and

ninety... it'd been a while. I saw the flyer that day in the

student center as thought it'd been placed there for me.

But I always checked the bulletin board.

It was a coincidence. Renita and I had been discussing other activities for me to get into. I was accepted into the organization I'd applied for a few weeks back. I was a part of a sisterhood, a service organization that was predominately Black and the largest of its kind on campus. They too, had a bit of a reputation, but I'd given it a chance in spite of. I met Ann and Pearl Ann that year through the organization. The three of us had become inseparable. I'd found out the two of them had gone to high school in Dallas together, so they'd known each other prior to college. We were a part of the same intake class within our org. Each time our organization took in new girls, people would liken us to a sorority, and for all intents and purposes, we were; right down to the drama.

I'd largely avoided that part. I was too busy having fun. I didn't tell my sisters my idea, but when I told Ann and Pearl I was planning to apply to become a contestant in this year's fall pageant, they supported whole heartedly. Pearl Ann even agreed to do it with me. The decision to take the risk had me tied up until I mustered up the courage to get a hold of the application. At the last minute, I'd reached out to one of the sponsoring fraternities' members. He'd seemed hesitant to give it to me, questions dancing in his caramel colored eyes. He'd *heard* about me. I could tell. That look had become so commonplace around campus that I almost relished in the infamy. They didn't *know* me, so why get worked up? My strong exterior was wearing though. The gossiping left me alone at night, wounded. I'd lost myself to confusion. The expectations of others had clouded my view of myself and I had to regain control. It was my life and no one was living it with me. I'd grown tired of suffering in silence.

Candidate interviews were held the same week I'd picked up the application. Dizzily, I found myself glancing, side to side, sizing up each girl. Some were tall, some thick, some shy. But all seemed more perfect than me. I'd put together my best outfit, a royal blue high waist skirt and red blazer.

"Candidate 8!"

Oh no. That's me.

Breezily, I walked into the room, smile in tow, as if I'd had no worry in the world. A few of the girls who'd finished their interviews before the group of hopefuls I'd been assigned to had relayed questions to us as they left, so I was somewhat prepared.

The panel of judges gazed intently at me, as though they all knew who I was long before I stepped foot into the room. Each step pulsed loudly in my mental as I made my way toward the lone seat before the judging table. The young man with the caramel colored eyes was there. Something told me that whatever suspicions he'd had that day he'd given me the application had been relayed to the other panel members. But I was already here. What was I gonna do? Leave?

"What's your favorite animal and why?"

"A Koala. Because I like to think that I'm cute and fun."

Silence.

"Where do you see yourself in five years?"

"Well, I hope to join the Air Force and use my training from college to secure a job teaching high school on base."

Crap. I lied. I didn't want to go to the service. I didn't

know what I wanted to do actually.

Keep going.

"How do you feel about first impressions?"

A male voice broke the monotony of feminine energy.

My eyes calmly motioned over to where the question had derived. It was him. Heat rushed to my face as the air in the room grew terse like they all had been wanting to ask similar questions.

I think first impressions are a term that simple minded people use to mask their judgment. I was livid. I'd opened myself up to this kind of judgment and for what?

What was I doing this for? Because I was bored? Couldn't be. Had that been the case, the last inquiry would have brought the entire interview to an end. Why was I there?

Why did I believe these people would change and give me a fair chance?

Breathing deeply and softly, I answered. "Well, sir, everyone is entitled to their own opinions. It is up to individuals to make decisions of those they encounter, so I can't say that I believe in first impressions. Leave's room for judgment, you know?"

~

I didn't get an email. Pearl Ann did though. I'd not been chosen as one of the contestants. I didn't know the exact reason why. All I knew was what I could assume and there was no use in being upset about that because as the saying goes "It is what it is". The scholarship money would have been nice, though.

Why did I never seem to be good enough? What was wrong with people? Why couldn't who I was suffice?

To them, I still wasn't good enough to sit down and have a conversation with.

A girl like me was only good for gossip and sneers. I just had to deal with it and move on. Pearl was in, so I would be happy for and support her.

The organization, as it turns out, had been good for me. Community service was fun. Giving back to others with my sisters often took my mind off of my own soap opera. Again, food had become scarce in my house. Majority of the time, if I was eating, Renita was providing it. Jobs were harder to find. I'd lived in small towns before, but it looked as though this one took the title. The college population grossly overwrought the city's, making the job pool even smaller. I had a part time waitressing gig, but business was fickle seeing that the restaurant was fairly new.

Faltering business meant tips were just as uncertain and with the debt I'd accumulated from the move, expenses prior to, and keeping it all a secret from my roommate, I'd needed my organization to give me something else to focus on.

Pearl Ann had been keeping me abreast of her pageant proceedings over the past few weeks. All of the coaches were members of sororities and from what I was hearing, it showed. The pressure from the coaches and the fear of performing in front of the entire campus had run off more than one contestant and the pageant was at stake.

"Yeah, another girl dropped out today." Pearl told me.

"What do you mean?" I replied in disbelief.

"I mean what I said. Another girl quit the pageant."

"But why, though?" I contemplated.

"You would think that people would appreciate the opportunity seeing that so many girls interviewed."

"Well, it's hard. Some people can't dance. Some people don't have a talent. Some people don't speak well in front of people."

See, Pearl Ann never had much to worry about. She was a technically trained dancer and well known for it on more campuses than one. Everyone loved her. She was five feet and three inches of fire. Her Black and Mexican lineage gifted her long, flowing, thick hair and with a saucy attitude to match; she and I both knew she'd be chosen. Only the public speaking aspect called for hesitation. But she was well capable of that too. Apparently, a few of the other ladies hadn't been so sure of themselves.

With three weeks of practice in the books and the pageant only four weeks away, the alarming decrease in participants left us both wondering what the fraternity would do to keep one of their staple events alive.

My answer came in the form of an e-mail from the chapter vice president:

"Upon further review, we would like to offer you a chance to be a contestant in this year's scholarship pageant. If you are still interested in participating, please respond within 48 hours of receipt of this correspondence.

Best wishes."

I read the message in amazement. *The absolute nerve of these people! How could you reject me and then, when all of your "perfect" candidates fall off, ask me back, as though I didn't know I was a backup option?*

The audacity of these people! To refute a great, potential participant and think she would want to be picked up after being canned like a 70's sitcom. Tuh.

"Well just say no then."

That was Ann's reply to the situation. She was always a black and white kind of person.

No gray area. It was simple.

If I had no desire to be anyone's second place, decline the invitation. But for some reason, I hadn't dismissed the idea. I hadn't said no. Mulling over the email had me really wondering why I'd ever applied in the first place. One thing I'd learned about myself after leaving J was although I rarely wanted to admit it, there was a reason for everything I did, good or bad.

I may not have always known at the time, but there was always a reason. It felt as if I needed to take the chance. I felt...obligated almost.

There I was, sitting in a pool of my own feelings; embarrassment, shame, rejection floating around me. Dissecting the source, I saw that all of what I felt, all of those emotions were tied to how *they* saw me. The same *they* who said I didn't qualify to begin with.

I'd been fighting the same stigma all of my life. It wasn't that I cared about what *they* thought; I just didn't understand *how* they thought. Who were *they* to say I wasn't good enough? Or anyone, for that matter. Before I'd applied to participate, I'd remembered hearing girls in the hallways discuss their own chances of being selected. *Girl, I'm too fat to do that pageant. They don't pick fat girls.* Or *I'd have to buy a dress. I can't afford that.* Or *I'm not pretty enough for a pageant, especially that one.*

There it was.

It made sense now.

It was as if God Himself had broken his vow of silent uncertainty. The words landed in my heart as though they were my own. I knew it had to be a higher power because I could never come up with something so timely, clever, and precise.

Your Purpose is Greater Than Your Pride.

I *had* to do the pageant. I knew exactly what those girls felt. Every woman knows what it feels like to simply not be enough, to have to forfeit a race she would never have a fair shot at. Yeah, I had been rejected, but so what? I got a second chance when so many others felt too low to even try for a first. I owed it to them. I wasn't fat. I'd always had the opposite problem. I had no idea how I would afford a dress.

My rent was past due. And pretty...well, that was a concept I'd never really known.

The entirety of my life had been filled with cruel jokes denoting the hue of my skin, the texture of my hair, or the way I pieced outfits together. Just as I was obligated to do this for other girls, I had to speak up for myself. That was the only way, the only time everyone would finally hear me. I settled the matter within myself. If everyone was going to have an opinion of me, I'd at least provide them the facts.

Over the next 4 weeks, I was forced to face every insecurity, even ones I didn't know I had, from the length of my arms to the way I walked. It was true; the pageant coaches had not even a hint of mercy. Two were also trained dancers like Pearl and one of the other contestants. The other coach was the queen from the year prior. But the head coach took the cake.

Verse, who was well known for her poise and impeccable articulation, became the worst part of Tuesday and Thursday evenings. The dancing was bad enough. I was the tallest contestant, so that meant I towered over every other girl. During portions of the opening routine that were meant to be sexy and feminine, I felt large. I felt like a bull in a china shop, ruining every piece of aesthetic beauty in sight. Oh, but when Verse showed up to practice, it was though the temperature in the room dropped from the frigid expression on her face. Her soft, gentle voice always cut a bit deeper than the others when she chided us.

"You know you guys look awful, right?" She'd begin.

Soft and matter of fact.

"I'm going to tell you if no one else will because I refuse to have y'all out there looking crazy. If you don't want to take this seriously, that's fine.

The door to your left is unlocked and you can, like so many others, see yourself out if you so choose."

I'd gotten a late start because of my second round status, so I had a lot of catching up to do and she took no excuses. She reminded me, as I started, restarted, and started my wayward pageant walk again, that I'd made the decision to be there. Regardless of my time constraints, I had to excel. Night after night my pageant mates and I walked the same patterns, recited the same introductions, and held the same poised, yet tortured smiles trying out different pairs of heels for our show padded by tube socks. That's one thing we all had in common. All of us were involved in our respective organizations and departments. Practice often caught the tail end of our meetings and events, so we would come "as we were".

Some days that meant tube socks strategically worn that morning to dull the ache of the heels later that night. Some days that meant hats when we were in between weaves or deciding to erratically dye our hair bright hues sending our coaches into frenzied panics and long exchanges in group texts…wait. That was me.

The pageant had drawn nigh. We were days away and I'd finally finished working on my talent. Sort of. My talent would be a poem that I'd started writing when I decided to enter the competition. After truly understanding my purpose for participating, I'd put all of my energy into that piece. I didn't worry about much else. Public speaking, that was easy. The dance? I had rhythm, I just had to commit to it.

But my poem had really taken shape over the course of the weeks.

Each night I would sit to write it, I struggled for the words. The delivery had to be dynamic. That meant I had to truly *mean* every line. Searching for meaning, I dug back into why I'd started this journey. I found myself penning issues that truly bothered me. Why had I come here and felt the pressure to fit in? That was not my norm. Why weren't many girls wearing their natural hair? I was no advocate for the lifestyle, just a participant. And I knew it had to get tiring always having to maintain a weave, hiding beneath caps on the way to class in between styling sessions. And makeup? In my mind, my skin was clear enough. I'd *seen* battles with skin conditions, so a blemish here or there never bothered me. I couldn't afford fancy hair and didn't know much about concealers and blushes, but what I did know, was that none of it mattered.

Every woman holds a special quality that makes her, her. I'd been judged by those same shallow standards of beauty for many years. The same *they* that'd told me I was ugly as a child now sang praises of my beauty. Surely, there'd been some type of transformation that'd moved me up in the ranks; a change that made me more beautiful than her or her or her. Nope. My skin hadn't lightened, my hair was actually a lot more nappy, and I had gotten taller over the years, which I'd heard, was unattractive. So what exactly made any of us "pretty"? If young women continued to listen, *they* would continue to feed us their false realities, their ideals of beauty, and we would never see what was so beautiful about us.

And what made me beautiful?

I was a good person and I'd worked really hard at that. It was genuinely never in my heart to harm anyone.

I exercised care in my dealings with others because I too well knew, words hurt.

They could harm people in ways that the eye would never be privy to see. I was living proof of that. 22, still fighting battles of insecurity from years' worth of pain turned scar. Words also had the power of healing. Over the past year, I'd made it a point to give compliments to others. Sometimes a kind word could really brighten someone's day, reminding me years ago of where I'd been and how perilously close I was to taking my own life from the strength of words. Yet again, I was fighting a battle over who I was, fighting to be me. I didn't want to be a model or have to have my face "beat".

I just wanted to do what I wanted to do and I felt that every woman should have that choice without someone in her ear telling her what's attractive, what's pretty, what will get her a husband.

If I wanted to wear sweatpants during the week, it was my choice. If I wanted to gather my hair in a messy coil on top of my head and leave the house with not a hint of make up on, again, my choice. But why did we not feel comfortable enough to make those choices?

The stage seemed lonely that night. Spotlight. I don't like. Blinding.

But pressed against the back wall I could see a sea of gold.

What a sight to behold.

We had worked so hard. All of the coaches had eased up as we progressed, even Verse. And tonight was the night. My dress was white with a sweetheart neckline and yards and yards of tool. I couldn't think of a more fitting color. I loved simplicity and elegance.

White provided both. I'd opted for a wig.

A friend from my college days in Oklahoma had recently been battling breast cancer and offered me one of her favorites to wear. I was grateful. I'd asked one of the girls at school to handle my makeup needs. As mentioned, I was no expert, but I wanted to look my best. My pageant mates and I all scurried around backstage to get ready. The room was littered with makeup brushes, stray shoes, and half dressed women looking for either of the two. Quietly, I observed the women who'd grown into my friends, each taking care in the way she looked. I was proud of us.

Just weeks ago, we had all seen our breaking points. Some of us cried, others...Let's just say my Sissy had to call on the name of the Lord more times than one in order to maintain the sanctity of her religious vows. We'd faced our deepest fears together, become friends through practice and sisters through pain.

I looked left and saw one of my new friends, Marie, crying. Pearl Ann walked over to see about her.

"I'm scared," Marie sobbed. "I can't do this."

Marie, although confident and prepared at practice, had always fought off the anxieties of standing on stage. It was her mountain to climb. Sissy, who had been doing her hair in a mirror against an opposite wall, peered back, curling wand in hand, to listen.

Upon hearing Marie's concerns, Sissy, with one half of her hair in a bun, the other cascading into beautiful spirals, sashayed over, hips and thighs bare. Sissy had a walk like a mother. You know? The kind where you know mama is coming to make it all right. She took Marie's hand from where she sat and she commanded the rest of us to the middle of the floor for prayer. We held hands, heads bowed, sealing our sisterhood in that moment as we prepared to walk onto the stage and leave it all there.

...would I be your type?

If I was the loudest girl in the room

Would you notice me then?

If I frequented Mac, Sephora, and only bought my hair by the bundle

[baby]

Would you think I'm beautiful?

When she wakes up in the morning

Looks in the mirror

What does she see?

The beauty of her skin or her minds capacity

Or does she see the freckles, the bruises, the spaced apart

eyes

The blemishes the bumps

Imperfections concealer can hide

How does she feel the day after she gave him her love?

Broken, defeated

Called his phone

Can't get him to pick up

Where is her smile?

And why can't she see

That she is more than her looks

Full of personality

You are your heart

You are your smile

You are your grace

You are your style

Daughter of Heaven, Mother of Earth

You are a Queen

So

Know your worth

See, I see the beauty in you despite how others may feel

about you

Know that everything you do, even the small things,

affects somebody around you

Like, shoutout to my plus sized girls

With the hips and the curves

They've shown me that I am not body

Don't settle for less than you deserve

And what's up to the female athletes

Running the track or picking up a ball

They've taught me that men may be good

But women, oh we can do it all!

And I can't forget my dark girls

With the skin that's brown and rich

We got to love this

Embrace it

But know that we are not defined by this

And sending a word of encouragement to all the girls

That have come to me and said

"I can't go to class today. Mm mmm! Not with these naps

on my head!"

Or

To the girls who are afraid to step out on their dreams

Because of lack of confidence or simply

because you have no idea what the outcome may be

To you I say this:

Step out on faith

Accept yourself

Cause if you don't

Won't nobody else

See I am who I am

I'm gone be who I'm gone be

And if you can't accept that

Then you can't accept me

And I never said I was perfect

That's what the world seems to forget

But one thing I will not do

Is live my life with regret

I am tall

I am dark

I am tatted

I am smart

I am different

I am me

After all who else will be?

Why fit in when you can stand out?

That's my motto.

That's what I'm about

Just be you

Who else is there to be?

Cause at the end of the day,

Oh, I'm gone do me.

My thoughts are good

And my advice

But I'll do you one better

I'll lead by example.

Chapter 6.5

2013 was looking to be a good year. I hadn't won the pageant (that interview question was a killer), but that'd never really been my intent. I'd had something to say. No crown could have given or taken that away. Plus, losing to Marie, didn't feel like a loss at all. Honestly, losing to Pearl Ann, Sissy, or Marie would have felt like a victory. We were sisters, so when one won, we all did. We had all since returned to our normal lives but always as "The Faithful Four". The pageant had really changed things. I was still talked about, only this time it was mostly in regards to my stellar performance. Day after day, just when I'd thought everyone forgot about what I'd done on stage, another person would come and congratulate me on a job well done.

Even the guy with the caramel colored eyes had gained a new respect for me after my debut. That night following the pageant, he and I had spoken at length about our dealings and misdealings with each other. I'd explained how I felt he played a part in the opinions of others about me and he understood. It was although the poem had opened up a more human side of him. Of many. Even Verse finally understood why I'd seemed so rebellious during the process. Her eyes welled with pride that night after I'd come off stage from the big unveil. Tears brimmed over as she and my pageant sisters held each other tightly. My words had resonated within the heart of the campus and as much as I hated to take any credit, I had to be proud of myself for having the courage to not only bounce back from rejection but leaving a lasting effect on so many people. One of which…was Nova.

Heaven Sent. Although there was no God in this. Heavens! Repent! Addiction crept slowly where emptiness had taken residence and there was nothing better than this. No higher high than Hi. Dawns forced for-ced goodbyes. Diving deep into our li[v]es. Blind Trust.

Nova had been at the pageant that night. My opening speech contained a quote from Kendrick Lamar and it'd caught Nova's attention.

"We all get distracted. The question is: Would you bounce back or bounce backwards?"

I'd meant that. I understood what it was like to be knocked from your square only to have to regain balance and try to press forward. Nova and I bonded over that common knowledge.

It was my first encounter with a male that I could actually see myself with. But seeing myself with him and being with him were two different animals; the latter of which I had no plans of encountering. There was no need. We were comfortable. We hadn't necessity for grandeur. The simplicity made it so fresh. We'd become each other's fresh air, mine of sweet countryside fragrance. It was all new to us both, but the adventure of exploring our unknowns aided in his progression and mine. I was familiar with ambition, but I'd never seen it before quite like I had in Nova. He intrigued me and I was addicted.

My sisters in service had seemed changed ever since the pageant. Though the majority gushed with warm congratulations, the overall front was a cold one, a chill I tried desperately to ignore. To make matters worse, our numbers had begun to dwindle. Service activities saw less and less effort and attendance.

Our president had done all she could to get the girls back on track, but collectively, we'd been damaged by arguments and attacks on each other's characters. The constant fighting had been enough to drive away a large portion of our members. The decline in work ethic, though, had bolstered mine. Although I had been committed the semester prior, I had still contributed to "the problem group" who was often blamed for a culmination of years of bad raps. Our girls as a whole had often been described as "wannabe sorority members" and "party girls". Neither title was without some merit as year after year had seen at least 3 members move on to a Greek letter organization and abandon ship and as far as the partying, that was the nature of college. Apparently, since we were a part of this illustrious organization, that was supposed to curb our behaviors as people for our name's sake. I'd heard the message the semester before, but it didn't really seep in until the spring of 2013. Hard work had become a memory and I couldn't understand for the life of me why one would apply to an organization, get accepted, pay money, and then just stop showing up. It was asinine, really. And then to commit to something, a cause where others depended on our efforts, and simply not be present with no excuse or explanation was far beyond me. But when I was out serving, none of that mattered. The way I saw it, there was no use in focusing on who wasn't there; just use the ones of us that showed and let the others face consequence. The only issue was, there was no consequence. Each meeting girls would brush away their absence with indifference as though we hadn't all signed up to do this. The room we'd gathered in weekly had become a war zone. Members had began to stop coming to meetings altogether while our president cheerily presided like nothing was wrong. I had to applaud her game face because these girls were absolutely out of line! Disarray finally caused chaos to ensue. Character assassinating comments flew left and right taking out anyone in their untimely path. Tensions boiled over as members began raising their voices and standing from their chairs.

That was my cue. I was never one for conflict and this had gone too far. Leaving the room, I scrolled down to his name and hovered over.

"Hello? Nova? Yeah, it got bad tonight. I'm tired of fighting just to go out and help people. I can't take this."

"Well D, if it's so much of a problem...run for president."

President? I'd never thought of that. I had never been in any type of leadership position before. You had to be a societal perception of perfection for that kind of thing. I would have to clean up my image. Did that mean no piercings? Hide my tattoos?

Would I have to stop going out? I loved hanging out and just being a regular student. But I didn't want to change. The whispers about me hadn't stopped entirely, but I'd found the source: my own sisters. The cold shoulder I'd gotten after the pageant was accompanied by stories of rumored encounters and truths about less than shining moments. It was like they were trying to tarnish the reputation I had created for myself since the pageant. Other students had come to me telling me of my sisters' betrayal, but I refused to believe the extent of their involvement. Why would they do that to me? I'd never harmed them. But if I was going to be president, I would have to lead them and to lead them, I knew that meant, yet again, opening myself up to criticism and the face of judgment.

The semester grew more tumultuous among us. I was one of the few who'd never stopped going to meetings. I decided to express my thoughts of presidency with the one person who had always been supportive of me: the current president. One night after a March meeting, I'd asked her off to the side. She had no idea what I was about to ask and approached with her usual chipper demeanor. Breathing steadily, I told her about the ideas I'd had to make our organization stronger, detailing a rewards system, more concise by-laws, and more engaging programming for the student body. I was proud of what I'd come up with and was certain that my president would encourage me to move forward with my pursuit of candidacy. But she didn't. She looked inquisitively into my eyes as I spoke, only denoting her reception with a grunt or a thoughtful sigh.

Puzzled, I immediately raised internal defenses. Something wasn't right here. How had she and I gone from unwaveringly supporting one another to what looked to be, now, a one way street? She began to speak, advising me of the changes I would need to make in my personal life to be accepted into such a position. She began to reveal everything that'd been relayed to her about me with certainty as though I'd come to her, myself, with the information. Staring intently, I listened as she berated me and gently explained every reason why I shouldn't run for the office. "Oh and then there's the issue of your grades," she stated.

How had she known about my grades? We were only required to provide an academic eligibility report in the fall semester. I wasn't even failing any classes. I may not have had A's, but since the pageant I'd actually given a bit more effort to my coursework.

Nodding politely and thanking her for her insight, I walked away knowing that this task would be more daunting than I realized. Before, I faced the student population at large, a crowd of people who knew of me, but mostly, had had no dealing with me otherwise. These were my *sisters*. We'd gone through the process together, attended weekly gatherings, hosted socials at each other's homes, laughed, cried, shared secrets; if no one else on campus had an idea of who I was, they did, so why had it seemed since the pageant that they no longer wished to have that connection with me?

I prepared my speech for a week straight. I never practiced reading it aloud, but I knew what I had to do. I had to be strong. Word had gotten out among our org (and the student population, too) that I was running for president. Ann was the one to nominate me.

No one else would dare. Although I had sisters who spoke ill of me less than others, they all had colorful comments about my lifestyle, body image, and reputation. And I'd known. Nova had taken extra care in letting me know just how capable I was. He was so strong. His frank and curt answers always left me feeling silly for having questioned myself in the first place, but how could I not? He was only one person and there were 30 members in my organization. *They all can't be wrong about me. I just want to help make us better. They'll see. I'll show them.*

The day of the election, I'd come into the student center prepared. I'd decided on a black top, cheetah print booties, and a pair of creased red dress pants that I hadn't been able to fit a few weeks back.

I rarely wore the color red. The boldness attracted eyes and even though I was always minded, I never truly was one for going out of my way to get attention. With quiet resolve, I took the elevator to the top floor, stealing a few moments to myself, stilling my nerves as I walked into what I'd already known would be an ambush. From the time I announced my intent to run, it had been an ongoing conversation among the group of ladies. I held my tablet firmly, reading over the words I had written for my toughest audience yet. As the double doors slid open, I put on my best walk. Returning my tablet back to my oversized bag, I let the bag rest in the fold of my arm, reverting back to my modeling days, taking on the open corridor, each step filled with a fierce, yet grateful confidence.

"I like those pants. Red is a power color. Looks good on you."

The compliment had come from a passer-by, a young man known on campus for his fearless and dapper style. I nodded with a tight smile, butterflies dancing in my stomach, but a face that read business.

Upon my entry into our regular meeting space, the air became still. Girls had already gathered for what was sure to be a show and everyone was looking my direction. I sat down like I'd not felt their stares piercing through me, as Ann, too complimented my choice of outfit. Red and cheetah print were her two favorite things in the world. I showed her my speech. She read it silently as hopefuls stood acknowledging why they should be chosen for this position or that. Chaplain to historian to secretary. Parliamentarian was up next. Ann had decided to run for that position, knowing that if I was elected, I would need a strong executive board.

She was unanimously voted in. Then came the last of the positions. The candidates for vice president and president were required to make a presentation outlining why they were the best selection for the job. Capability-wise, I'd known no other girl could do what I could, but the odds were not in my favor a my turn to speak finally came.

Reading my speech aloud, I thought to myself how great I sounded. Here I was, running to be one of those elite student leaders I'd seen the semester before when I'd first transferred in.

In less than a school year, I had watched a transformation happen. I wasn't totally changed and that had to be the most rewarding feeling. I was unashamed of my truth, confidently proclaiming what I had to offer when years ago, I hadn't even been able to look at my own reflection. My sole visible tattoo spoke volumes across my wrist, reminding me of how I'd landed there in the first place.

Faith. As I finished my speech, smiling at a job well done, I looked around the room. I mean *really* looked around the room. The faces of my sisters had become stern and hard as they listened to me speak. I wasn't sure if they'd perceived my speech as lies or if something more menacing was at work. Either way, I was ready.

"Where do you see the future of this organization under your presidency?"

"I believe that we can build on the foundation we've set here. Although this year didn't go the way we planned, it did move, and for that, we must give ourselves some credit."

One question down. I think I did alright.

"What types of events would you like to see presented on campus?"

"Education is why we are all here. I believe there is a decline in educational programming because it's not engaging to the students. If we can introduce stimulating programs that also inform, I think that'd be a step in the right direction."

That sounded really good. Ok, Self!

"Do you believe that your personal reputation will harm the reputation of our organization?"

Here we go...

"Well, I believe that we have all been victims to the he say/she say rumor mill. I can flourish in this position with the help of my sisters. That said, we can't worry about others' perceptions of us. We have to work hard and accomplish the goals we set out to accomplish and all of that extra, won't even matter.

That was the most diplomacy I had.

"We often have events will male organizations on campus, do you think that anyone would be able to take you seriously as president especially considering how much you go out, stay out all night, and whatever else you're doing in out here?"

Excuse me?

That question launched 45 minutes of torrential degradation with everything from who I'd been seen with, who it was rumored I was intimate with, and my attendance at some of the more exclusive off campus events up for discussion. If I told you I was shocked, I'd be a lie. I already knew what type of people I was dealing with shortly after the pageant. It'd taken a long time to come to terms with the idea that sisterly only meant support when the playing field was level.

As soon as the rest of the campus stopped seeing me as a bad girl, a few of my sisters worked overtime to keep their version of the truth alive.

As the ladies took terms taking aim at my heart, I thought back to the countless nights we'd stayed up together playing board games or the past Christmas break when three of my sisters and I had a week long slumber party at my house. I remembered who'd kind efforts turned into cutting glances and who had just had stop speaking altogether. I didn't understand, but I didn't care to. Hurt people, hurt people. All I had to do was love them. Love them beyond pain, love them beyond fault, just show my sisters that no matter what they did, I would forever love and care for them because that what loves does. It forgives.

The summer began the changing over of ranks. I'd won the presidency. It didn't feel much like a win though.

Our end of the year celebratory banquet was so uncomfortable I'd left early sensing that many weren't too happy about my new position, although they'd voted me in. I'd known the climate of our group when I'd accepted the office, but I stayed encouraged. Through my love for service and hard work, I would set an example, getting us back to the strong coalition of women we were known to be years back.

Ann was my new parliamentarian. Actually, the entire exec board was now made up of sisters from my incoming class. We "new girls" had taken over as some of the older, problem members started to graduate and subsequently phase out.

Our chemistry was a bit rough, but we had the makings of a good, solid leadership. Throughout the summer, Ann, the other exec board members, and me all tried to talk about issues that'd come up that past school year.

One glaring flaw was our set of by-laws. Arguments ensued that past year over the wording of the governing rules especially when a sister found herself in hot water and needed to get out of trouble. Because I'd been an English Education major, I thought it best that I go through and outline the loopholes and grammatical errors that'd played a part in our conundrums and have a revised copy of the by-laws ready for review upon the date of my first official meeting as president. We weren't, as a whole, very orderly, so I had to get us on task. You have to start how you want to finish and in disarray is not where I wanted to start.

My ideas all sounded great to me, but I'd decided to run a few of them by sisters I was close with who were not on the board. I wanted them to feel included in the process; even though I held a position now didn't mean things changed. I still wanted to be at movie nights and sister socials. I was no different than them and I wanted them to know that. We worked and developed a couple of ideas for programs based off of the voting the all of us had done the semester before. I built their ideas, the exec board's, and my own into an outline of how the school year would go. We would leave it to the general membership to decide the details so that they were able to really get hands on and enjoy the event process. If they did not agree to what had been put together, they would be able to simply vote it down, and the exec board and I would start over, garnering suggestions from the members until we were all on one accord.

That was what my summer had become, getting on one accord. My student worker position and my organization were my only commitments which not only gave me time to dive head first into my work, but to reflect internally.

I had to figure out how I would lead such an impassioned and strong willed group of women. A group of which, largely, felt unfavorably towards me. It wasn't my first time being disliked, it was, however, my first time having to be a leader to such a group. Was the love in me strong enough to withstand their jabs and covert insinuations? The answer was yes. I'd known that from the day I'd announced my run for the highest elected office in the chapter. But had it seemed that I had the ability to love beyond doubt, fear, or reproach? *Searching.*

Before I left Oklahoma back in 2012, I'd began dabbling in the readings of Jack Kornfield. I'd been introduced, by a friend, to his specific kind of knowledge. When I first got a hold to his book, "A Path with Heart", I'd studied it as though it were my cheat sheet for a major exam.

Many nights as J lay sleeping, I would be awake, highlighting passages that sounded interesting or made sense. Some of his words had been answers to life's most challenging questions, however, most had gone over my head. I couldn't understand some of the principles he taught. Fusing them with my own beliefs also had been difficult. I reopened the book that summer of 2013. Each day for about two weeks, I would read as much as I could digest and process. The greatest aspect of literature is its vague, yet concise nature.

We are open to interpret any work of literature as we so choose, deriving our own meaning, giving it new life. The work of an author never really dies.

One of Kornfield's opening chapters discussed "Taking the One Seat". The phrase hadn't made much sense to me the year before, but this reading birthed a new insight.

As it stood, the organization depended largely on me. Our fate was hinged upon my demonstration of mental and spiritual fortitude. I had to be strong. Given what I'd been through over the past few years, I'd already done a multitude of things I'd once thought I couldn't. There was a strength in me that sat just beyond my reach, constant doubt, mostly doubting myself, blocking my view. I needed to find out what made me dynamic as a leader and embrace the fact that I had a good heart and good intentions and roll with that.

Over the years, few understood the better portion of my actions; how I was able to take J back after what he'd done or why I hadn't retaliated when the young lady he'd dealt with keyed my car. It just was not in my heart to harm anyone. My life was proof enough that I could withstand pain. But the pain that caused people to wrong one another was far greater than any pain I could inflict or allow myself to feel and for those people I only wished healing. I knew what it meant to hurt, to want to hurt every thing and everyone around you; I understood some people weren't able to bear that kind of pain. I was. So I would. I would consume my sisters' deepest insecurities, seeing past the outer shell of physicality, and smolder that darkness with light. I turned to meditation to learn to harness the love that took home in my heart. In order to keep them positive, I had to remain positive. I pulled out my blue yoga mat and lit my incense. The scents calmed me as I steadied myself for what was sure to be an arduous task. Motionlessly, I sat on the floor working to quiet and control my thoughts. I never thought it was possible. My mind had always raced. Doctors told me it was one of the symptoms. My thoughts though, were productive, they were mostly just ill timed. I decided to dissect my life, my own fears and pain piece by piece. To give them my best, I had to be at my best; that meant confronting the pains of years past that had left permanent scarring to my body, my soul. *Pain.* Eyes closed, I focused on that word: pain. What did it mean to me? How had it manifested itself in me? Who had I become in its name? Slowly I breathed in the feeling. My body filled with pressure from the immense amount of air I had begun to take in, subdued by the feeling. I called to mind the tears I'd worked so hard to hide, the feelings I'd convinced myself I no longer had. And I cried. I wept.

Tears of relief cascaded down my cheeks as I'd taken the time to sit in my own emotions. The pain couldn't hurt the same way twice, actually, it didn't hurt at all. That day I acknowledged that my life hadn't been what I'd thought it to be. I had allowed my pain to mold who I was. Everything I was, was the product of energy sent in my direction and I'd received it, not realizing the power of what I was ingesting. It occurred to me, if I could learn to control my thinking, I could control the energy around me. All it took was for me to do was what I'd always done: love. Love is strong enough to overcome anything. It was innate for me to love others. I'd done it all my life; dying daily to offer up a kind word even when I hadn't one for myself. But if I was going to be the best I could *to* my sisters, I was going to have to be the best I could *for* myself.

Love Yourself. Or Nobody Will.

Chapter 7

My first meeting as president lasted over 3 hours.

That morning, I'd left home leery, but confident that I was ready to handle my new responsibility. I took care to get dressed in a black and white dressed and 5 inch black heels. I hadn't anything lower. My makeup was soft and for the first time, I think I'd done it right. Natural colors worked best on my clear, brown skin and I was content. I felt pretty. I searched for my phone as I'd made a habit of haphazardly laying it around, disconnecting with the world if only for a moment. It was time for me to venture onto campus and get things prepared for our meeting that night. Finding my phone beneath the couch cushion, I noticed the text message icon on the screen.

I opened the message. It was my advisor.

"The meeting has been moved to the room adjoining my office. Be there at 6pm."

Did she just *tell* me *my* meeting was moved…in a group text?! I didn't even get a chain of command courtesy? As I walked out of my front door, I saw how the year was turning out to be and braced myself accordingly.

Our initial August assembly was filled with questions, objections, and abstentions as sisters wasted no time interrogating the executive board. I wasn't sure if it was the sound of my voice, the color of my dress, or the new agenda format but they charged forward in the name of bettering the organization.

My fellow leaders sat beside me, though. I'd warned them that an incident like this might happen, but none of us expected the powder keg to explode so soon.

Looking at the faces of my cabinets members, I could tell they were flabbergasted by the volley of malice masked as productive criticism; productivity being the last word to describe what was going on in there. We sat through the interjected suggestions, side conversations, and challenges of authority until the advisor finally came in and put a stop to things. I wasn't surprised by what happened. I just didn't understand why they didn't like my ideas. I'd thought they were great ideas, efficient ones even. We could cut costs here or scale up there, change our promotion style… Change was good, I thought. My sisters didn't share the sentiment.

Autumn brought about transition. School was back in full swing as freshmen transitioned into college and upperclassmen moved off of the scene.

I, for one, had less time to go out and lose track of time fiddling with friends. The college parties had been fun, but I had obligations now. I made time for fun around those obligations. Relationships with the members of my organization had transitioned too. The discord continued each week no matter what the topic. My spirituality was going to be tested; that was a definite.

Nova was back from summer break and I was happy we'd picked back up. He visited a few times over the break and that, too, had surprised me. His company relaxed me on the most stressful of days. He'd always been candid with me about everything.

There was a joy, an inexplicable joy, in that. By this time I'd settled into the idea that I was president of this organization and it was going to be hard. That was just a given. Other thoughts plagued me. The student center had begun a hiring spree that subsequently left the older employees with less hours.

I had a system. I was just getting somewhat stable, meaning the electricity had only been disconnected once that season. That was an improvement for me.

As surely as that silver lining came, it went. The balancing act of being a student, a student leader, and a student worker forced me to prioritize and, of course, the student aspect was the lowest on my list. How could you be a student if there wasn't enough money to cover your costs of living?

Focusing on school while battling eviction was a mental state that I'd no intention upon seeing again, so I'd resolved in myself, if push came to shove, I would leave school. Nova supported my decision, but wanted me to finish. He began requesting extra hours at his job to be able to help with small expenses such as gas, food, and internet.

I'd never had anyone do anything like that before. He'd done it as though it was his responsibility. I guess you could say, for all intents and purposes, he was the man in my life. I appreciated that. I needed that. Sometimes I would come home from class and he would already be inside of my apartment, resting comfortably on the couch or making himself a plate from food I'd prepared the night before. The nature of our relationship had shifted in its intensity.

At first, our exhilaration came in the form of secret trips and cryptic text messages in case anyone would see, but who would? We both had at least two locks and a secret storage on our phones. Lately, our focus was mainly on our respective organizations, our grades, and keeping each other balanced. He kept me level headed when the theatrics of my sisters were too much to bear. Every Monday evening, I would come home, drained. Keeping a smile in the face of bitter criticism was daunting. I was starting to wonder how bad I really wanted this presidency. It was like there was no reasoning with them. No matter how much sense I thought I made or bases I thought I covered, someone always had a complaint. And if they didn't, by the next meeting they would.

Too much goodness cannot reside within the nature of sin. For when it does, man cannot believe it so. Such is the nature of the human condition.

xD. Milan

"Keep your eyes open, sis".

It was a heeded warning from one of my executive board members. From what she was telling me, there were rumors circulating that a few sisters were looking to "get me out" of office. Never in the history of our chapter since its inception in 1997, had anyone been impeached. Never. I'd heard my chaplain's warning, but gave it no more energy than that of a watchful eye. *Oh great. How far are they gonna go with this?* I had to wonder. Their disdain seemed to know no boundaries and evidence of that showed more and more by the day. It was exhausting and I was getting too old for indirect confrontation. Funny, because years back I'd been too afraid to even let anyone know they'd hurt my feelings.

I was 22 now. I was a grown woman with bills to pay, a man to tend to, and had no space in my life for passive aggressive attitudes.

Meditation brought much clarity as to my desires. Emotionally charged, I was sensitive to the energy of others. Positive or negative, happy or sad, it was like I could feel it within feet of my approach. Secluded sitting had also equipped me with a no nonsense attitude. I'd learned the reasons so much had hurt in my lifetime; I also learned to recognize the warning signs. This was for the sake of keeping myself grounded and my path clear of anything that did not serve to benefit my future. Still, though, my carnality begged to know the root of the problem. Was it an inability to handle business? It couldn't be. Since I had been president, we saw record numbers in attendance and fundraising.

Events that usually averaged us $700 in proceeds skyrocketed to $1200. I had always been prompt and professional in my exchanges whether digital or face to face. That only left one other option: these girls had a personal problem with me. Their concerns were relayed to my advisor as though the integrity of the organization as a whole had been compromised because of my business ethic *and* my personal interactions. One complaint that was I was being asked to do quite a number of events featuring my poetry at events run by fraternities. They'd expressed concern that other kinds of relations had been the cause for my success. It was also stated that I was manipulative in my approach with the girls, only filtering information I thought relative while secretly fulfilling my own agenda.

What agenda? Who even thinks that way?

Turns out, my sisters did and they were willing to tell their story to anyone who would listen. Meetings became crusades to stake their claims, war to tarnish my already fragile image. Finally, one day, I couldn't take it anymore.

"Call the vote," I stated simply.

"It has come to my attention that a few of you are looking to have me removed from office. Look, the way I see it is this, if we are fighting every step of the way, we are only getting away from our true purpose of helping one another. In addition, I don't stand for gossiping. We left that behind with the last era. Now, if I am going to continue presiding, I would like to do so peacefully, without the interruptions of you," fingering one member who had been disrespectfully rebellious the entire semester, "or you," I finished pointing at her cohort.

I'd known exactly who was behind the sedition and I had no problem letting them know that I saw them for exactly who they were and through exactly what they'd planned to do. They opened their mouth to protest as I raised a gentle hand, stopping them.

"Call the vote."

Ann looked in my direction, almost as if she were proud. She slowly turned to our equally reactive membership. Looks of shock, guilt, and uncertainty crossed the opening of our empty square table arrangement. Four tables sat in a square, facing each other, and I, sat unmoved. If the girls had put enough effort into their plan to change the others' mentality toward me, their plan would succeed.

13 in favor, 4 oppositions, and 7 abstentions with 6 members absent. I was still president...for now.

The opposition came even stronger after the vote. I'd roused a couple feathers with my "arrogant" decision to bring my own position into question. I hadn't thought it arrogant at all. I was honestly just tired. I was sick of fighting with people I loved, and who knew I loved them, to do a service of love for others. Bottom line, I wanted to bring quality programming to our student body and gain a wider visibility for our organization. We were one of the last few thriving chapters left in the state. No amount of bickering could change the greater goal here. But what good was I if they didn't want me there. It was evident that they had no plans on ceasing their efforts.

Information concerning my academic status had somehow become common knowledge. At the time of my election that past April, I had been sitting perilously close to the GPA threshold. That May, I dropped below it.

I enrolled in summer courses to retake classes and take care of my grades before officially taking office that fall.

How had they known about that? No one was privy to all of our grades, but the executive board. There had even been a campaign at the beginning of the semester to keep grade reports out of my hands. Seems I wasn't the only one with questionable qualifications, but I'd obliged to make them comfortable. Pick your battles. That confidential information was now spread among my sisters and, although I was not ashamed, I knew it would be one more reason I would be deemed unfit.

Nova remained objective.

"They will do their best to impeach you. Are you prepared for that?"

I had to come to terms with the reality that the one thing I loved the most was about to be taken from me. If the girls had gone that length to inquire of my academic status, they meant business. The hatred for me had grown so strong that one of my sisters even tried to fight me on campus. I stood calm, as I watched her face transform into someone I didn't even recognized. Those nights we'd cried together, vowing we would work through her insecurities together and renew our bond had been forgotten.

The sleepovers, late night swims, and home videos were all distant memories as I watched everything I'd work for fall apart around me. Yes, it was irrational. Yes, there may have been a chance we could have worked it out, but they were beyond that.

I knew it.

I faced them for the last time. I knew that Monday would be my last as president. I felt it. When I walked into the room, more than one member had bulleted notes in front of them. I found out only minute before the meetings, those papers had been printed, outlining my shortcomings as president. I also noticed the presence of members who hadn't been present since the opening weeks of school. My advisor was also present. She had made it her business to be more present this semester to "mediate".

In resilient silence I sat, as the girls I once called my sisters assassinated everything about my character, my caliber of work, and who I was as a person. In their most professional attire, they berated me and belittled all of the hard work I'd invested into our beloved sisterhood. The floor was again open for voting.

This time, the advisor thought it'd be more appropriate and unbiased to vote on all positions. We decided as to not intimidate anyone or make any one person feel uncomfortable, we would write our votes down on tiny slips of paper for the secretary to count. One by one my executive board was voted back in with no objections; Historian, Chaplain, Secretary, Treasurer, Ann, and the Vice President. When it came time for the presidential reelection, I, unlike the others, was asked to step out of the room. I agreed. I mean, it wasn't like it would make a difference anyway. We had been voting on tiny slips, so whether I had been in the room or not, I couldn't see how anyone voted anyway. I stood across the hall in the lobby, watching as the sun began to set. I couldn't believe I'd come this far just to have it potentially taken away. I loved serving the community. I felt like I'd found my calling. I'd even incorporated my own nonprofit that summer. My heart felt at home when I was able to give to someone else. I remembered those times where I had no steady income with no certainty of a meal that day. I knew the added struggle of working and still not being able to afford textbooks. Compassion was a part of who I was. I had the gift of empathy. My own experiences gave me the ability to truly understand someone the way we all want to be; the gift of listening beyond just hearing. All I wanted was to share those gifts with others, to give someone an experience with a genuine person.

My secretary peeked out of the door motioning me to come back inside. The decision had been made. With a majority opposition, I was removed from my position as president of our chapter.

I nodded gracefully, thanked my sisters for the opportunity to lead them, and gathered my belongings. The voting procedure had been changed in my regard. There were no slips of paper. Once I'd left the room, there had been a minor discussion prior to the vote and the ladies were then asked to vote by show of hands. Anonymity devoid to all…except me and I'd had no desire to know anything other than the number of abstentions. The sound of the door closing behind me brought a bittersweet aching to my stomach as the elevator doors closed on that chapter of my life.

Although, I'd been prepared, nothing could quite steady me for the pain that'd come after my dismissal. Not only had I been impeached, some of the girls had gone bragging to their friends about how they'd finally gotten rid of me.

I was embarrassed. I knew it was the biggest scandal on campus that semester. Everyone went back to whispered conversations of me. Some felt my sisters had done the right thing by getting me out. But the general consensus was that it was a very distasteful situation. I started receiving messages from other leaders who vowed to never do business with my group again if I asked that of them. I couldn't do that. I wouldn't. I'd never be a hindrance to the legacy of an organization I respected so much. Some of my executive board members took the change hard. Two stepped down from their positions, one of which left the chapter permanently. It was a mess. I was a mess. I couldn't bear to be at the student center.

The magnitude of the drama warranted unprecedented attention and questions. Whether it was to be nosy or just to get the inside tip, I couldn't take it.

I needed to sort myself out. I hadn't seen the inside of the belly of pain in so long, but sadness have overcome me and engulfed every semblance of light I had left. For the first time ever, I'd felt like I had purpose. My life had become greater than me. I let my pride give way to my purpose. I didn't regret it, though. My stepdad always told me not to give away nothing I couldn't afford to lose. That didn't just apply to money; time, energy, love, those are abstracts we can't replace. I loved freely. I never regretted loving them. I never cared about who was right and who was wrong. I just wanted them to see how beautiful they were, how capable they were. There was never any need for comparisons or competition.

Grief had overcome me so, that I couldn't see Nova. I wasn't ready to be vulnerable with him on this. He already had my heart in the wake of my lost love, I couldn't allow him this too.

I needed to do what I'd set out to do back in 2012: lean on myself. I had more time on my hands; that was good. I needed it to heal. That time in conjunction with my already decreasing campus presence aiding in my recovery process. The actions of the girls hadn't been the most hurtful part. What hurt the most was being stripped of something I loved so much by people who didn't care. They'd questioned my commitment, my integrity. Calling Ann was the most contact I had with the outside world for about two weeks after. I had to be sure that I wasn't losing my mind and that I had done all I could to make things work.

"Taking the one seat" took on a new meaning for me. I could only be responsible for my own actions. Worrying about why the girls would willfully hurt me with no regards to how it may affect me could not become my being.

Spiritual development became my focus. I would make certain I handled everyone with care, even if that meant I lay damaged.

October brought additional hardships. The extra staffing at my job had not been accidental. Word had gotten to me that a supervisor wasn't too pleased with my performance and had plans of letting me go; this, however, relayed to me by a student who wasn't a worker for the department; not a campus worker at all. I had my own theories for his interest in my termination. Sure enough I was called to his office and fired, citing a three write up termination (two of which were given at the same time).

My only other source of income was a stipend that I received from my father's status as a disabled veteran.

He had done his full 20 years in the army and retired. He applied for disability and after some pushback was able to secure a 100 percent status. For me, that equated to a governmental stipend that aided in the costs of school and living and on October 1, 2013 that all came to an end.

I didn't know much about politics, but I knew back in September at the mention of the possibility of a government shutdown that I'd be one of those affected. Getting in touch with Veteran's Affairs was harder than trying to ring God's direct line.

The wait times were hours long in the days before the shutdown. Apparently, I wasn't the only one who was nervous of their uncertain future.

I waited day after day, hour after hour hoping someone would be able to ease my mind and assure me that my check would arrive on time. It didn't.

And after October 1st, there were no employees in the office to address the concerns of the veterans, spouses, and dependents. Dejected, I thought about all I'd lost in such a short time. I'd been robbed of the presidential position I'd worked so hard for and I was fired two months shy of my one year anniversary with the student center. I had nothing left to take; nothing left to give. My only escape involved escaping into myself, avidly searching for the remains of my lives.

From state to state, bottom to top and back to the bottom again, I looked up knowing I had no place to go. The rumbling in my stomach reminded me that elevation was my only option.

The actuality of my situation set in. With my birthday approaching, I hadn't much to celebrate. Even if I'd wanted to do something special for myself, I simply didn't have the money.

Experiencing poverty had never been as unkind, but the fall quickly turned into winter and with no money and no food I still had to muster the strength to maintain my obligations and look bravely into the faces of those who'd betrayed me. They'd thought they won. I was bloody and bruised, but unbroken. My time in Oklahoma had steadied me for the encounter

I started working at a local pizza franchise. At least, this way I'd be able to eat. Every night I came home to a stillness I never experienced before. Life was alright. Even though everything wasn't perfect, they never would be. I wondered what my next move would be as I entered 2014, but Nova seemed to have a hunch.

"2014 is going to be your year. Just watch."

He'd said it often after the impeachment.

Some days he laughingly referred to how I would be able to look back at the year's events and laugh at the turn of the tables. Some days he said it with so much conviction I wondered if he'd somehow been privy to my fate. The affirmation felt good. It fit. 2014 would be my year.

Chapter 8

In January, I received my first awards for community service. Although my personal nonprofit was small and my presidency was short lived, the service I'd done hadn't gone unnoticed. I was awarded the Spirit of Commitment award from the county I'd resided in as a college student. I, later that month, received another award. This one, the MLK Scholar award, came from an adjoining county, honoring my commitment to academia, positive strides towards change, and a forward thinking leadership mentality. I'd never received anything like that before. Up until my initial election as president, I hadn't done much worth mentioning. What *had* I been doing all of my life? The exhilaration that came with leading others and making change could not be replaced.

I was even more motivated to continue my pursuit in changing lives. So what if a few people didn't see the vision? It wasn't for them to see. It purposed for *me*.

Nova had made a very important statement at the end of my first and last term in office.

"If you were the problem in the organization, it will show. They will get better without you. If not…"

Knowing I'd given my all, making a conscious effort to support my sisters and my community, gave me peace of mind in the months after my impeachment. A couple of the girls toyed with the idea that I would be too angry or embarrassed to show my face at meetings during second semester. Boy, were they wrong! Although I was unhappy about what had happened, it was the past. I was confident that I wasn't totally at fault for the cacophony and that I had, indeed, been the best for the job.

Having exercised my skills, I'd discovered many talents I had never even known I had. I had a knack for event planning; every detail from the time and date of the event to the types of favors for guests was a chance to practice my creative flair. The girls had mistakenly thought I'd fallen in love with power. As I'd told them before, if they could accuse me of such, they'd never truly known me to begin with. We can't wrestle with those who don't understand us. Sometimes, who we are isn't meant for everyone to understand. Sometimes, the true lesson in the situation is in that revelation alone: knowing that you're set a part, knowing that you will never fit in, becoming resolute in that fact. I still supported my sisters. It hurt my human, yes. But I had to rise above that carnality and tap into the agape love indigenous to my spirit. So, yes I went back, the very next meeting encouraging my sisters and the new presidential appointee as we fought to climb.

The spirit honored my efforts. My father drove down from Oklahoma to see me receive my initial award. Shaking hands and taking pictures with the president of my university was a dream come true. Never did I think anyone would notice me and, nonetheless, for doing what I loved! *Did I just say loved?* My passion had been awakened. In harmony with my spiritual guide, my temperament grew mild. The world looked different. The air smelled different. And my eyes, my eyes were open. The haze dissipated right before me.

Feared cliché, life had new meaning. Motivation wasn't just a word anymore. It became tangible. My job at the pizza place was paying the bills. I was a delivery driver. That meant, often I was delivering on campus to my peers. I didn't care. I couldn't care. I took pride in my favorite khaki pants, slip resistant, black low tops, and apron that sat against my hips.

Working there had always given me food to eat, so I'd finally gained that extra few pounds I always wanted. I was ok. I could finally breathe.

Breathe.

breathe

breathe.

Breathe life into me. Anew. A new. I knew.

Time escaped. Only regained in age.

Maybe we've all been here before…

Time had gotten away from me. School had become routine and checking into credit hours since the transfer had always set me back a little emotionally. A friend, who was close in age but much more studious than I, called me asking if I could come see her at her office.

She worked in administration and often helped me when I was searching for answers, loopholes rather, regarding school policy. When I met her, she asked if I knew how close I was to graduating. I didn't. I'd honestly, just grown used to the habit of struggling to attend class. As time had it, if I took a summer course or two, I could graduate in December. I was in shock. So much happened over the past two years, I'd lost track of the ultimate goal: graduating.

Leaving her office, I pondered the end of my time there. What would I do? What kind of career did I want to get into? School had provided more questions than answers regarding my future. Accepting who I was, fully, meant accepting the facets of me that didn't agree with societal standards.

Why should I have to live my life like everyone else's? If that were the case, I wouldn't have had to break my back to pay for class, or go hungry for days, or as an adult, glue my shoes together, just to give the illusion I had it all together. (Ha, I made a funny). Nobody lives the same life. A 9-5 had been the source of bouts of depression throughout the years and I simply couldn't take it. I had to accept that too. So what would I do?

My pizza job had been good to me, but I was offered a summer position on campus to supervise youth camps. The job included free room and board. I'd never lived on campus at either of my schools, but I knew the opportunity would afford me a break from rent and utilities. My landlord knew of my financial struggles and was more than willing to let me out of my lease.

No penalty! Since the year's beginning, the stars had been aligned in my favor. Seamlessly, I was able to move from one job to another and from a tough living situation to something a little lighter. I'd had a roommate before, so meeting Emerald and seeing how pleasant she was proved to be a sign for an amazing summer.

Just like I thought, my new employer took care of us. For the first week of our stay they had meals and games for us, the residential staff, form relationships and get to know each other. A few other staffers were personal friends, so I'd never been alone unless I chose to be. My room was housed in one of the best facilities on campus with a beautiful courtyard view I gazed out at every morning and night. My blinds were never closed. Bathing in sunlight and basking in moonlight gave me peace in my temporary residence.

Relations with my classmates were minimal as I was spending the majority of my time with the people who mattered the most; close friends and Ann. The past spring semester, I'd watched one of my dearest friends, Eugene, walk across the stage and into his destiny. He was the educational type. Higher education was his calling and he'd seemed so sure. His graduation brought me to the realization that I wasn't too far behind and a master's program wasn't on my list of things to do.

I sat at the receptionist desk in my dorms, watching the comings and goings of campers, as my job description outlined. Lecie, Emerald, and Remy, all co-workers, sat next to me giggling away at the latest antics from the kids.

"Did you hear them running on the second floor last night?" asked Remy.

"Girl, yes!" Lecie responded. "I almost went up and got them all the way together!"

We all laughed.

Emerald and I had our own dealings. I'd taken my summer to live freely. Each day I was either walking the town in the early portions of the morning or I had, otherwise, found myself engaged. Emerald, too, had a life of her own. She and I were barely in the building to notice, but we knew that specific camp had been a handful.

"Guys, I graduate in December." I spoke softly with my head bowed.

A slight sadness came over me with each word. I would miss this life. I had grown to not only love, but understand my journey, and the end was near. The next phase of my life hadn't even been a thought until that day.

Knowing I was interested in nonprofit work, I bounced

the idea off of the ladies. Squealing in delight, they all

spoke of how they could see me in that field.

"You've always loved saving folks!" Remy joked. "But I

think you'll love that."

She was right. Ever since the fiasco with my

organization, I had worked harder to reach out to others.

Back in March, I had organized a clothes drive under my

own nonprofit, partnering up with Ann and a group of her

friends back in Dallas who also did charitable work. July

also promised to be eventful as I readied myself for a

success seminar that I'd organized in Oklahoma City. I

was a featured speaker along with three others I knew

would go on to do great things. I loved nonprofit work

and planning events.

True to my nature, I took the advice of the girls and looked into positions I'd enjoy upon my imminent graduation. Maybe it was too soon to apply for jobs, but at least I would be prepared. I didn't want to leave school with no prospects and I definitely didn't want to go backwards after I'd made so many forward strides financially, so I applied for jobs that would pay for my relocation and offered a generous salary.

I was stunned to receive a call back in early July. "If you're interested, we would like to offer you the position of Marketing Manager for our nonprofit organization in Atlanta, Georgia starting this August."

Atlanta???

August???

That was the next month! How would I…what would I… That was the next month! I still had furniture from my apartment in storage and…no job or place to live after this summer program. The timing was uncanny. How was it that the universe had dropped a job into my lap at the same time I was wondering where I would go for the fall semester? Wait. If I took this job, how would I finish my last semester? Did I physically *need* to be in Texas to finish? If I took that position it provided me the motivation I needed to finally finish college.

It was all solved. Every tear, every fear, and every emotion I never thought I would recover from had all made sense. It was like I had been led this point, almost pushed into it. If I moved, I could use the financial aid money along with my stipend to get settled while completing my coursework online.

I'd outgrown it there in Texas. There was much bigger and better ahead for me and I felt it. The start of 2014 indicated that and there was no way that a college student who hadn't yet graduated should have snagged a job like this.

I thought of where I would live in Atlanta, how my life would turn out, and I couldn't see much further than August. It didn't matter. Faith had made way for me so many times before. When I couldn't pay my rent…faith. When I had no food to eat…faith. When I'd lost the positon as president…faith.

Somehow, there was always way out. Somewhere beyond my control lie the life I'd always dreamed of. Remember, "So as a man thinketh, so is he," and not once had I ever seen myself not "making it". Whatever that meant for me, I never knew failure.

I may have known disappointment or "things didn't go as planned", but I'd never encountered failure and with that mindset, I accepted the position anxious for the next part of my life's journey.

-D. Milan

The End x D. Milan

I saved this part. I saved it until I was done. Six months, I dedicated to exploring myself, finding myself in hopes that I could reach you.

Yes you, Reader. See, we can't really reach others until we deal with our own struggles and I knew if this meant enough to me, that the pain, like it had so many other times, would be worth what I found.

As I write this letter to you now I am currently four days late on my rent. I lost my car after a February accident on a rainy evening and my job on April 5, 2015. I have had to take the bus back and forth for over two months to the public library and the APEX Museum to write this book because I could not afford a computer and I recently found out that I missed my graduation threshold by .1 causing me to have to retake a class to earn my diploma.

See, I knew, in order for you to *hear* me, you had to

know that I understand. I understand your pain, your

plight, your fear. I used to live there.

We cannot burden ourselves with the things in life that

don't take shape the way we imagined. Had I done that,

we wouldn't be here now.

Rather, use each day as a learning experience.

Building upon the facets in our lives that we can change,

rejoicing in the positives.

Who knows? Maybe I'll sell enough books to pay for this

last class.

But at least I took the first step…

Trying.

Until Next Time, Friends.

About the Author

D. Milan is Atlanta-based author who dabbles in various other styles. Known in the south as a journalist, D. decided to venture into authorship in hopes that her debut novel "When We Were Young" would impact the community and gift people the desire to read. She is also a songwriter and avid traveler, taking any opportunity to express herself creatively and gain new experiences. Deemed the "shy socialite" D. is a presence of light and freedom, known for her quiet demeanor. Her favorite activities include updating her website, ByDMilan.com, with new music and content and exploring new cultures.

"Wisdom is not the acquisition of knowledge. It is knowing that you can never acquire it all."

-D. Milan

Acknowledgements

Wow, this feels strange. Like an acceptance speech almost, so I'll keep it brief. I have to first give honor to God and the universe for conspiring in my favor. Nothing feels better than this moment. I would also like to thank Dan Moore, Sr. of the APEX Museum for guiding me to and through this process and making sure I ate.

May Kate...my sweet angel, we did it.

If you were mentioned in the book, thank you. Whatever our interaction, good or bad, helped me get here and I appreciate you for helping me become a better person. Jacob Waddy on the cover shot. You did that boy! Fleur, my dear heart, your kindness will not go unnoticed. You are blessed and your mother is proud. Draven, thank you for listening to line after line, night after night. You're the real MVP.

Jimmy and Liz… thank you for your encouragement. Ann… you know I love you girl. Bae Brown, I'm clutching my pearls! We did everything we said we would! Dad, thanks for paying my rent more times than once. I told you I was doing something great. I just stick to it and forsake all else in it's name. Briggette Woodard. Mom. Dad. My nieces, Titi loves you!

And to everyone who has supported me, my readers, my fans…every message has brought a tear to my eye. Every copy I sell is for you. Let this be your motivation. We can do anything we imagine. Just Dream Big!

-D.

© 2015 Desiree Jefferson